New Directions for
Student Services

Elizabeth J. Whitt
EDITOR-IN-CHIEF

John H. Schuh
ASSOCIATE EDITOR

Strategic Directions for Career Services Within the University Setting

Kelli K. Smith

EDITOR

Number 148 • Winter 2014
Jossey-Bass
San Francisco

STRATEGIC DIRECTIONS FOR CAREER SERVICES WITHIN THE UNIVERSITY SETTING
Kelli K. Smith (ed.)
New Directions for Student Services, no. 148

Elizabeth J. Whitt, Editor-in-Chief
John H. Schuh, Associate Editor

NEW DIRECTIONS FOR STUDENT SERVICES (ISSN 0164-7970, e-ISSN 1536-0695) is part of The Jossey-Bass Higher and Adult Education Series and is published quarterly by Wiley Subscription Services, Inc., A Wiley Company, at Jossey-Bass, One Montgomery Street, Suite 1200, San Francisco, CA 94104-4594. POSTMASTER: Send address changes to New Directions for Student Services, Jossey-Bass, One Montgomery Street, Suite 1200, San Francisco, CA 94104-4594.

New Directions for Student Services is indexed in CIJE: Current Index to Journals in Education (ERIC), Contents Pages in Education (T&F), Current Abstracts (EBSCO), Education Index /Abstracts (H.W. Wilson), Educational Research Abstracts Online (T&F), ERIC Database (Education Resources Information Center), and Higher Education Abstracts (Claremont Graduate University).

Microfilm copies of issues and articles are available in 16 mm and 35 mm, as well as microfiche in 105 mm, through University Microfilms Inc., 300 North Zeeb Road, Ann Arbor, Michigan 48106-1346.

SUBSCRIPTIONS cost $89 for individuals in the U.S., Canada, and Mexico, and $113 in the rest of the world for print only; $89 in all regions for electronic only; and $98 in the U.S., Canada, and Mexico for combined print and electronic; and $122 for combined print and electronic in the rest of the world. Institutional print only subscriptions are $335 in the U.S., $375 in Canada and Mexico, and $409 in the rest of the world; electronic only subscriptions are $335 in all regions; and combined print and electronic subscriptions are $402 in the U.S., $442 in Canada and Mexico, and $476 in the rest of the world.

EDITORIAL CORRESPONDENCE should be sent to the Editor-in-Chief, Elizabeth J. Whitt, University of California Merced, 5200 North Lake Rd. Merced, CA 95343.

Cover design: Wiley
Cover Images: © Lava 4 images | Shutterstock

www.josseybass.com

Contents

Editor's Notes

D r. Jack Rayman published the most recent *New Directions for Student Services* sourcebook on career services, *The Changing Role of Career Services*, over two decades ago. Our hope for this sourcebook is to provide a more current perspective reflective of a new context. While many of the imperatives presented in Rayman's (1993) publication are still relevant today, much has changed and the role of career services within higher education is not exactly the same. In fact, it is a fascinating time within our field. An expectation for transformation by campus leadership—often without the commitment of new resources—is the primary underlying theme when our career services colleagues gather. That was the case before the President's College Scorecard focus on college outcomes developed, and expectations have only heightened since then. More than ever before, university career centers play a key role in higher education. It is therefore critical for those within the profession and those making policy related to career services to understand its central importance. Part of the need for this particular volume is to help educate university decision makers on the current context and importance of career services.

This volume provides an overview of emerging trends for career services and identifies strategic directions for the profession, coupled with practical advice. It is written at a time when challenges for career centers are greater than ever before considering the changed landscape in higher education and the world of work. Throughout the country, the merging of—and in some cases elimination of—career services reflects how the profession is at a crossroads. Yet the importance of career services is, perhaps, greater than ever, and career services professionals are not necessarily equipped with training to "tell their story" and make the case for its critical role and future imperatives. Additionally, it is important for professionals within the field to remain current with strategic directions, learn from best practices, and have an opportunity to be the ones to "tell our story."

The chapters in this volume blend research, case studies, and personal experiences of the authors and are intended to stimulate a productive dialogue about career services. I selected the topics for this volume based on conversations with colleagues and readings over the past several years. While less than systematic, these topics seemed to be of interest to practitioners and those in university leadership roles. The authors offer an expertise in their respective topics, either through research, prior publications, or having heard them in well-received conference presentations. I am confident that they have a great deal to contribute to the ongoing discussion about career services and am forever grateful to them for their contributions to this volume.

New Directions for Student Services, no. 148, Winter 2014 © 2014 Wiley Periodicals, Inc.
Published online in Wiley Online Library (wileyonlinelibrary.com) • DOI: 10.1002/ss.20104

In Chapter 1, Farouk Dey and Christine Y. Cruzvergara frame the volume with the chapter "Evolution of Career Services in Higher Education," in which historical and emerging trends in university career services are described.

In Chapter 2, Jeff Garis discusses how career centers can offer value-added services to their institutions in forging partnerships; how they should be leaders in creating university-wide, innovative career programs and systems; and the central role career centers play in that mission. This chapter is titled "Value-Added Career Services: Creating College/University-Wide Systems."

In Chapter 3, Keri Carter Pipkins, Gail S. Rooney, and Imants Jaunarajs focus on the core value career counseling still plays in today's context, the need for ongoing counselor professional development, and practical "best practices" for us to use for such development in the "Back to the Basics: Career Counseling" chapter.

In Chapter 4, Katherine E. Ledwith provides an excellent overview of a topic much discussed within our field: collaboration between career services and academic advising. In the "Academic Advising and Career Services: A Collaborative Approach" chapter, Ledwith offers suggestions on how the two entities can better partner to serve college students.

In Chapter 5, Julia Panke Makela and Gail S. Rooney explore the ever-growing focus on assessment within career services. In "Framing Assessment in Career Services: Telling Our Story," readers are offered a strong case on why assessment in its various forms is crucial to helping us "tell our story" to demonstrate value and for continuous improvement. In addition, the authors share strategies and resources.

In Chapter 6, "Career Services in University External Relations," Seth C. W. Hayden and Katherine E. Ledwith outline the growing role career services plays in university external relations.

In Chapter 7, Mark A. Kenyon and Heather T. Rowan-Kenyon write on the forward-thinking topic of how career services can play a key role in the internationalization of higher education in "The Globalization of Career Services."

A wonderful benefit of the current context is that significant attention is finally being brought to our field that I expect will spur innovation and change. I am convinced that preparation of our students to enter the world of work will improve, and in the end, that is why those of us in this profession chose the work we do every day. We are ready for the expectations for change. My hope is that universities, public and private, put resources behind their desire for transformation, and that this point is not lost in attention-grabbing headlines. It would not be fair to our students of today or tomorrow. I argue our field does not need to "die" but rather needs attention and authentic support to become a university priority.

Doing so may require a mandate at the highest level of university leadership to garner support for the understanding that career success of our students matters and is everyone's business. In addition to motivating colleges and universities to become more transparent with employment outcomes, hopefully the College Scorecard will also aid with the latter requirement.

I want to take the opportunity to thank two individuals who helped make this sourcebook a reality. One is my life partner, Chad Smith, for taking on more than his share in our relationship and care for our girls so that I could dedicate time to editing in the midst of a career and cross-country family move. The other is John Schuh; it has been an honor to work with such an esteemed colleague in our field, and I will be forever grateful for his wisdom and patience throughout this process.

I trust that this volume will help stimulate ongoing conversations about the roles, models, and best practices of career services in higher education. Best wishes to all involved with this field as you continue working to impact the career success of your respective students and alumni.

Kelli K. Smith
Editor

Reference

Rayman, J. R. (Ed.). (1993). *New Directions for Student Services: No. 62. The changing role of career services*. San Francisco, CA: Jossey-Bass.

KELLI K. SMITH *is the director of University Career Services at Binghamton University in upstate New York.*

Socioeconomic changes, technological advances, and generational trends have been the impetus behind every major paradigm shift in the delivery of career services in higher education during the past century, including the one taking shape today. This chapter will provide an overview of the changing nature and emerging trends that are shaping the future of career services in higher education.

Evolution of Career Services in Higher Education

Farouk Dey, Christine Y. Cruzvergara

Career services in higher education has evolved since its inception and adapted to various models following economic conditions, trends and demands of the labor market, and needs of the university and society. In the early 1900s, there were vocations bureaus, created to help new immigrants find work. In the 1920s and 1930s, vocational guidance for teachers emerged out of the need for more teachers. In the 1940s and through the 1960s, the need to match GI Bill veterans to jobs allowed for new job placement centers to emerge on college campuses. The 1970s and 1980s brought career planning and counseling centers, which focused on helping students and graduates explore careers and plan their own job search. The information technology and social media revolution of the 1990s and 2000s later transformed career centers into dynamic networking hubs that engaged hiring organizations in campus recruiting and facilitated networking between students and recruiters.

Each paradigm shift in the delivery of career guidance in higher education was connected to changes in economic, political, social, generational, and cultural norms. The economic downturn of 2008 and its aftermath changed the landscape for higher education once again, raising questions about the value of a college degree and engaging all stakeholder communities, including alumni and parents. What will be the new paradigm for how universities help their graduates' transition into careers? Figure 1.1 illustrates the historical evolution of career centers in higher education since their inception in the 1900s and predictions for the future.

New Directions for Student Services, no. 148, Winter 2014 © 2014 Wiley Periodicals, Inc.
Published online in Wiley Online Library (wileyonlinelibrary.com) • DOI: 10.1002/ss.20105

Figure 1.1. Evolution of Career Services in Higher Education (Cruzvergara & Dey, 2014).

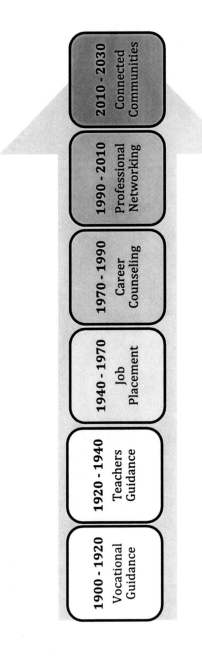

Historical Overview

Selected aspects of the evolution of career services are discussed in detail in this section.

Vocational Guidance and Teachers Guidance.   Before there were career centers on college campuses, faculty assumed the responsibility of mentoring their students and preparing them for future employment (Herr, Rayman, & Garis, 1993). Career guidance in higher education can be traced back to the emergence of vocational guidance in the early 1900s and the creation of Frank Parson's first career center, the Vocations Bureau, in the Civic Service House in Boston, MA, a public service entity that helped new immigrants transition to life in America (Vinson, Reardon, & Bertoch, 2011). In the 1920s and 1930s, industrialization and a post–World War I baby boom created an influx of students, which increased the need for educational and vocational guidance for graduating teachers (Vinson et al., 2011), slowly moving faculty away from their mentoring roles. Vocational guidance still remained absent in more than half of colleges and universities in the United States (Pope, 2000).

Job Placement.   The landscape of higher education and career guidance changed once again post–World War II in the 1940s and 1950s. A booming economy and greater employer demand for candidates juxtaposed with the need to place graduating war veterans who returned to college on the GI Bill accelerated the transformation of vocational guidance into the placement paradigm and the expansion of placement centers in higher education (Casella, 1990). Using Parson's trait-and-factor theory as a theoretical foundation, placement centers were responsible for matching graduates' abilities and interests with job criteria (Kretovicks, Honaker, & Kraning, 1999). Driven by a reactive approach and philosophy, and fueled by the increased demand for workforce in manufacturing and mining, career staff played the roles of job fillers and measured their success by placement numbers.

Career Counseling.   In the 1970s and 1980s, as higher education shifted into a development model, which placed the responsibility of learning and educational outcomes on the student, a slowing economy and increased competition for candidates changed the landscape for career services once again (Kretovicks et al., 1999). This paradigm shift forced students to take ownership of their own career development and job search, and recruiters to manage their own "matching process." This allowed career centers to step back into the guidance space with more emphasis on counseling, career planning, and job search preparation (Casella, 1990). The self-actualization movement of the 1970s and 1980s continued to strengthen the counseling model in career services, which heightened the clinician identity among staff and shifted the director's profile from a placement manager to a counseling supervisor. As a result, measures of success became less about placement data and more about appointment and workshop attendance counts. This would last until the next socioeconomic paradigm shift.

Professional Networking.   In the 1990s and 2000s, the dot-com boom increased the competition for candidates on college campuses, which helped reengage career centers in employer relations and helped transform them into comprehensive career services offices that facilitated the relationship between students and employers through various networking career events and recruiting activities (Dey & Real, 2010). New information technologies accelerated this process through the continuous development of recruiting software, and social media began to redefine how students make meaning of their experience and connect with employers and professional communities. With less funding from universities, corporate partnerships and revenue generation became a critical goal for many career centers, which further shifted the focus for career services from counseling to employer relations. The need to justify career centers' budgetary requests to universities also helped change assessment measures from attendance numbers to learning outcomes.

Connected Communities.   The economic downturn of 2008 has created an ideal environment for another paradigm shift in college services. Driven by increased pressure and demand for accountability from students, parents, alumni, faculty, and even government, many universities began the process of reinventing their career department, moving them from the traditional transactional model of career services toward a customized connection model that promises specialized career development support to students and meaningful connections to internship and employment opportunities as well as mentoring and experiential learning. As a result of greater investment in career services, career and professional development continues to become a significant element of the student experience rather than a resource that they seek when they approach graduation. Although the career center continues to offer career counseling, résumé assistance, and career fairs, its new iteration offers a stronger emphasis on building connections through partnerships with employers from a variety of sectors, experiential learning, mentoring, and developing career communities of learners and networkers that will engage students and alumni for a lifetime. In this new era of employability accountability for colleges and universities, the assessment focus will continue to be about first destinations and lifelong professional outcomes.

Emerging Trends

Similar to the last four paradigm shifts of college career services in the 20th century, the current transformation in career services requires the acquisition of additional resources, elevating the leadership of career centers to higher levels of influence, designing new and creative organizational structures, and establishing stronger coordinated campus partnerships.

NEW DIRECTIONS FOR STUDENT SERVICES • DOI: 10.1002/ss

Elevation of Career Services.   Senior leaders in higher education are beginning to recognize the direct link career services has to recruitment, retention, and revenue for an institution (Ceperley, 2013; Education Advisory Board, 2012). As a result, many are elevating career services, giving their leadership more institutional influence and the ability to convene internal and external stakeholders in order to help students leverage the power of the university network. Elevation includes changes to titles, reporting lines, and resources.

While leaders, regardless of titles, need to exercise savvy leadership to gain buy-in and demonstrate value, positional power adds a layer of systemic and organizational support that is also necessary to elevate career services in higher education over time. Titles for many leaders in career services are beginning to take the form of assistant/associate vice presidents/ provosts, deans, and associate deans. Recent examples of elevated college career services include University of Chicago, Stanford, University of South Florida, University of Virginia, Wake Forest, and William and Mary. This change has allowed institutions to more accurately represent the scope of responsibility and accountability placed on career services. Uniquely positioned as one of few units within a university that must actively engage with all academic deans, senior leadership, boards of trustees, advancement, the external community, and other campus partners, the upgraded title further illustrates the institution's support and value for career services. The change in title indicates a level of significance, accountability, and relevance to the university and to internal and external stakeholders. Similar to the evolution of admissions and enrollment management, it is our prediction that over the next couple of decades career and professional development will continue to be elevated and eventually sit as its own division reporting directly to the president or provost and serving on the senior cabinet.

As a result of title changes for leaders in career services, many institutions are adjusting reporting lines and merging offices. While the majority of career offices still report up through student affairs (National Association of Colleges and Employers [NACE], 2014), more institutions are considering new reporting structures to other divisions, such as academic affairs/provost office, alumni relations, advancement, and enrollment management. Recent examples include Seattle University's career services merging with academic advising, University of Chicago's career advancement moving to enrollment management, University of Richmond's career services moving to alumni relations, and University of California San Diego's career services moving to advancement. To be successful, such changes in reporting structures must be handled carefully, with the full consideration of institutional circumstances and engagement of all stakeholders and without compromising the integrity of professional standards.

Because of elevated titles, leaders of career services are typically reporting directly to the vice president of their respective division or to the provost. This direct connection to senior leadership gives career services a seat at the table with more exposure and more influence on the factors that will impact student success. In addition to changes in reporting structure, institutions are also considering strategic mergers to combine career and experiential learning opportunities, career and academic advising pathways, and career and alumni connections. These new reporting lines create opportunities for aligning institutional goals and embedding career development into the students' experience in a more seamless manner.

As institutions across the country look for better ways to prepare students for postgraduate success, the most strategic universities are investing heavily in a centralized career education model that maximizes resources and cuts redundancies. With greater visibility and accountability, institutions that recognize the value of career services have started to increase the amount of resources allocated for additional staff, increased operational funds to support programs and technology, grants or seed money to start new initiatives, and fundraising support for a new or renovated space that is prominently located on campus. Institutions are recognizing the need to more fully resource career services in order to better meet the needs of their constituents, to work more collaboratively with deans, to more adequately engage employers and alumni, and to develop more career-ready graduates.

Customized Connections and Communities.   Gone are the days of transactional services and general career information. Instead, new levels of expectations have emerged requiring career services professionals to redefine their value proposition for a larger group of stakeholders. With extensive amounts of information easily accessible on the web and through mobile devices, students and employers in particular are looking for customized information that will be specific to their needs or desires. By focusing on authentic relationships with stakeholders, career services professionals can transform their offices into hubs of connectivity and provide more tailored advice, strategy, and feedback to their constituents.

The ability to build these strong connections leads to the creation of customized career communities that better support student success. Recent examples of career communities include Stanford, William and Mary, and Miami University. At Stanford University, frequent career meet-ups, which are informal discussion circles guided by career counselors who are assigned to various student communities, are replacing the traditional workshops and presentations. In an era of information overload, students turn to their trusted network of friends, family, and advisors to help them cut through the noise. In order for career centers to best connect and serve students, it is critical to focus on building relationships with the people they trust, their inner circle. Creating customized communities allows for multiple networks to overlap and for reinforced support to guide students through their college and postgraduate experiences. By convening stakeholders across campus and beyond, career services can bring employers, alumni, faculty, families,

New Directions for Student Services • DOI: 10.1002/ss

Table 1.2. Continued

PARADIGM	1940–1970 PLACEMENT *Reactive*	1970–1990 COUNSELING *Proactive*	1990–2010 NETWORKING *Interactive*	2010–2030 CONNECTIONS *Hyperactive*
Director Profile	Placement director	Director: senior counselor, staff trainer, and supervisor	Executive director: manager of operations, employer developer, and fundraiser	Elevated role (AVP, VP, Dean): visionary, strategic and political leader, convener of stakeholders, and change agent
Reporting Line	Student affairs	Student affairs	Student affairs and academic affairs	Enrollment management, advancement and development, alumni relations, academic affairs, and student affairs
Location	Placement office	Counseling office	Web, classroom, and event hall	Mobile, social media, and hot spots
Employer Recruiting Strategy	Demand	Selective	Experiential learning (early identification)	Branding and campus engagement
Industry Growth	Manufacturing and mining	Retail and service	Technology, finance, real estate, and government	STEM, energy, social impact, healthcare, and media
Measures of Success	Placement data	Appointments and attendance at programs	Learning outcomes, engagement, and generated revenues	Employability: first destinations, reputation, and engagement

References

Bailey, M. M. (2014, June). *Differentiation steps to attract millennials.* Presented at the NACE 2014 Conference, San Antonio, TX.

Carlson, S. (2013, April 22). How to assess the real payoff of a college degree. *The Chronicle of Higher Education.* Retrieved from http://chronicle.com/article/Is-ROI-the -Right-Way-to-Judge/138665/

Casella, D. A. (1990). Career networking—The newest career center paradigm. *Journal of Career Planning & Employment, 45*(3), 33–39.

Ceperley, A. (2013). Changing times for career services. *Leadership Exchange, 11*(3), 24–29.

Contomanolis, M., & Steinfeld, T. (2014). Thriving in the brave new world of career services: 10 essential strategies. *LinkedIn Pulse.* Retrieved from https://www.linkedin .com/today/post/article/20140506211935-3053599-thriving-in-the-brave-new-world -of-career-services-10-essential-strategies

Cruzvergara, C. Y., & Dey, F. (2014). 10 future trends in career services. *LinkedIn Pulse.* Retrieved from https://www.linkedin.com/pulse/article/20140715120815-31028715 -10-future-trends-in-college-career-services?trk=prof-post

Dey, F., & Real, M. (2010, September). Emerging trends in university career services: Adaptation of Casella's career centers paradigm. *NACE Journal, 71,* 31–35.

The Economist. (2014, April 5). Is college worth it? *The Economist.* Retrieved from http://www.economist.com/news/united-states/21600131-too-many-degrees-are -waste-money-return-higher-education-would-be-much-better

Education Advisory Board. (2012). *Next-generation advising: Elevating practice for degree completion and career success.* Washington, DC: Author.

Herr, E. L., Rayman, J. R., & Garis, J. W. (1993). *Handbook for the college and university career center.* Westport, CT: Greenwood Press.

Kretovicks, M., Honaker, S., & Kraning, J. (1999). Career centers: Changing needs require changing paradigms. *Journal of Student Affairs at Colorado State University, 8,* 77–84.

National Association of Colleges and Employers (NACE). (2013). *Creating a strong employer brand. Spotlight for recruiting professionals.* Retrieved from https://www .naceweb.org/s07242013/creating-strong-employer-brand.aspx

National Association of Colleges and Employers (NACE). (2014). *NACE 2013–2014 career services benchmark survey for colleges and universities.* Bethlehem, PA: Author.

Pope, M. (2000). A brief history of career counseling in the United States. *Career Development Quarterly, 48*(3), 194–211.

Vinson, B., Reardon, R., & Bertoch, S. (2011). *The current status of career services at colleges and universities: Technical report no. 52.* Tallahassee, FL: Center for the Study of Technology in Counseling and Career Development.

Farouk Dey *is the associate vice provost of Student Affairs and dean of Career Education at Stanford University.*

Christine Y. Cruzvergara *is the director of University Career Services at George Mason University.*

New Directions for Student Services • DOI: 10.1002/ss

2

This chapter addresses a range of core programs that career centers can lead in contributing to an institution-wide seamless system of career services.

Value-Added Career Services: Creating College/University-Wide Systems

Jeff Garis

It seems like everyone wants to become involved in delivering career services in higher education. Academic advising increasingly offers "developmental advising" and career coaching. Many academic departments control internship programs. Often, academic colleges create decentralized career services and recruiting programs including career days and on-campus interviewing (OCI) without involving career centers (Garis, 2013). This chapter builds upon the Garis (2013) essay, "The Value Proposition," included in *Leadership in Career Services: Voices From the Field* (Contomanolis & Steinfeld, 2013), and, in using additional continua, discusses how college and university career centers can offer value-added services to the institution in forging partnerships with a range of departments and colleges including academic advising, academic programs, alumni association, student leadership and engagement, the registrar, corporate relations, and student affairs departments.

Career centers should be recognized and respected by their institution as *the leader* in creating college/university-wide career programs and systems. Value-added career services must address the decentralization–centralization continuum and how career centers can "friend raise" in creating innovative dynamic programs.

To be regarded as adding value to the institution, career services offices must begin with a solid internal infrastructure including a clear mission, supporting comprehensive programs, and a commitment to customer service. A well-defined mission with comprehensive programs can in turn be clearly communicated to the respective college/university community. This chapter begins with a review of four models or continua associated with the mission for the delivery of career services in college or university settings followed by a brief outline of core programs commonly associated with comprehensive career services.

NEW DIRECTIONS FOR STUDENT SERVICES, no. 148, Winter 2014 © 2014 Wiley Periodicals, Inc.
Published online in Wiley Online Library (wileyonlinelibrary.com) • DOI: 10.1002/ss.20106

Figure 2.1. Career Center Continua.

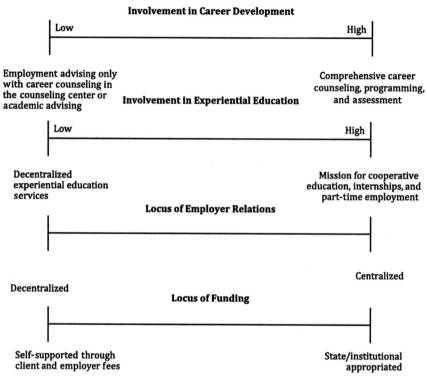

The mission for the delivery of career services in college or university settings can be categorized in four continua (Vernick, Garis, & Reardon, 2000) as outlined in Figure 2.1.

The first continuum reflects the degree to which the career center holds the mission for providing career development services with supporting career advising, counseling, assessment, and information. At many institutions, the mission for career counseling and administration of career assessments resides in the student counseling center rather than the career center. In such instances, the career center may provide assistance with employability skills but does not offer programs for academic/career choice or career indecision. Career centers with this mission would fall to the left of the continuum. At other institutions, the mission for counseling and assessment for career choice may be shared with a variety of offices including the student counseling center, academic advising, and the career center placing such offices in the middle of the continuum. In order to be regarded as comprehensive, the career center should shoulder a strong mission for advising, counseling, assessment, and information supporting career decision making, placing them to the right of the dimension.

The second dimension addresses the degree to which the career center holds the mission for providing experiential education services such as externships, internships, and cooperative education programs. Part-time, work–study, and volunteer or summer job programs could also be included in the continuum. Many institutions have internship or cooperative education programs residing in academic units rather than career centers, placing them to the left of the dimension. Commonly, the institutional mission for delivering experiential education is blended with colleges, academic departments, financial aid, and career centers all involved in these programs, placing them in the middle of the dimension. Fewer schools located to the right of the model have career centers shouldering the complete mission for experiential education programs. However, experiential programs including internships have always been regarded as among the most important powerful career programs contributing to student professional success. As a result, to be regarded as comprehensive, it is important for career services to, at least some extent, include experiential programs in their mission.

Employer relations services shown in the third continuum range from decentralized to centralized. Many institutions have decentralized career offices residing in academic colleges placing them to the left of the dimension. Other institutions have primarily centralized career centers charged with the college- or university-wide mission for employer relations and recruitment programs. Schools may fall toward the middle of this dimension through a hybrid model with the university-wide career center providing campus career and recruiting services in partnership with specialized academic college or department-based career programs.

Finally, the degree to which the career center is funded by the institution can be plotted on a dimension. At some colleges and universities, the salaries and operating budget for career services are not funded by the institution, causing career centers to generate their funding base completely through charges and fees to students' alumni and employers as well as fundraising efforts. At other institutions, career centers enjoy the full support of their institution for their operating budget, and any fees or contributions are used only as enhancement funds. Of course, many career centers will fall on the middle of the dimension in receiving institutional funding for staff salaries and some measure of central funding for operations but cover additional operating expenses through auxiliary-fee-based programs.

College and university career services falling at least near the middle and to the right side of the four continua reviewed earlier would generally be considered to be comprehensive, adding value to the institution and reflecting an institutional commitment to career services.

Core Career Programs

It is imperative that career centers hold the missions described earlier and provide supporting comprehensive programs as a foundation to offering value to the institution. Additionally, core "basic indicator" programs associated with comprehensive career services offices would commonly include:

- Assessment and computer-assisted guidance.
- Career education outreach programming.
- Career fairs.
- Career information.
- Career planning classes for credit.
- Experiential education and internships.
- Individual career counseling by appointment.
- Intake or drop-in advising or counseling.
- Job listings and résumé referral services.
- On-campus interviewing.

However, this foundation can be regarded as *necessary but not sufficient* to be considered a value-added career services office. Also, the commitment to customer service both for students and employers demonstrated by the career center in offering programs and services will contribute significantly to the offices' identity and value throughout the institution. Career offices regarded as value added are recognized for their energy, creativity, technological applications, and welcoming environments that include drop-in services.

The next level of value that the career services office can offer lies in our ability to assume an institutional leadership role in creating college/university-wide core career programs. Examples of college/university-wide systems that can be led by career centers follow. Additionally, because career services will vary in the extent of its involvement in the following, each of the career-related systems will be presented on a continuum as were the core missions. In order to avoid assumptions of the relative importance of any system, the continua are presented in alphabetical order.

Alumni Career Program and Systems.   Over the past several years, schools have increasingly been concerned with continued career support of their alumni. Accordingly, several models for alumni career services have evolved with varying degrees of involvement with the institution's career center. Some sample alumni career services delivery models include:

1. entirely sponsored and delivered through the career services office,
2. entirely sponsored and delivered by staff reporting to the alumni association, and
3. joint sponsorship involving staff and programs from the alumni association and career services office.

A value-added career center should be involved in the creation of the institutional system to address the career needs of its alumni. Joint sponsorship of alumni career services including staff with a dual reporting

Figure 2.2. Alumni Career Program Continuum.

Alumni Career Program and Systems

[_____]

No career services provided to alumni   Career center sponsored
through the institution   alumni career services

relationship with the career center and alumni affairs falls near the center of the continuum in Figure 2.2 and represents a particularly attractive institutional system for delivering such programs.

Career Day Systems.   Career fairs are among the most visible recruiting programs at most schools. Here again, the organization and sponsorship of career fairs fall on the decentralization/centralization continuum (Figure 2.3). Increasingly, many career fairs are outside of career services' control and sponsorship. However, the career center may recommend an institutional system of career fairs that may include a range of sponsorship options: (a) career services sponsored, (b) joint sponsorship with career services and departments/colleges, (c) departmental/college sponsored with career services' administrative/software support, and (d) department/college sponsored with follow-up interviewing conducted/scheduled through career services. Also, the career center can take the lead in chronicling and communicating the array of all career fairs offered within the institution to students and employers. Finally, as career fair activities (e.g., employer registration and student participation) serve as excellent barometers and indicators of the strength of recruiting activity at the college or university, the career center may want to collect and report activity data regarding all of the career fair events held at the respective institution even when some of the events are not sponsored through career services.

Career Development Credit Courses Systems.   Many career services offices offer credit career planning courses. These courses can become quite visible and systematic within the institution (Figure 2.4). For example, the career center can take the lead in organizing a course and creating the syllabus yet include other professionals from academic departments in serving as instructors. Additionally, credit career planning courses represent a wonderful opportunity for instructional partnerships between career

Figure 2.3. Career Fair Continuum.

Career Day Systems

[_____]

College/department/student organization   All career days sponsored
sponsored career day events   by the career center

Figure 2.4. Career Course for Credit Continuum.

Career Development Credit Courses Systems

[_____]

No career development credit   Career development credit
courses offered   courses led through the
                                                career center

services and academic advising. In short, rather than controlling and teaching very limited sections of a career development course each year, the career center can lead in creating multiple career-related courses and sections taught in various academic programs and involving varied instructors. In leading such credit courses, the career center strengthens the partnership with academic affairs and adds to its institutional credibility.

Career Information Resource Systems.   There are many online systems available that support student career development including occupational information, employer databases, career planning assessment and guidance, international career and employment information, and interview preparation/practice (Figure 2.5). Even in decentralized institutions, the career services office can take the lead in purchasing selected products and making them available to all majors college/university wide. In some cases, highly visible online career resources can be included in the secure login page for the institutions' academic support software application. This area can also offer an opportunity to collaborate with the university library system.

Career Services Recruiting and Administrative Support Software Systems.   Almost all career centers rely on software vendors to support their recruiting programs. These systems offer components that support some of the main recruitment services offered by both large and small career centers. Career fair registration and management, on-campus interview scheduling, job listings, résumé books, and employer/student databases are core elements found in such software systems. Of course, this dimension is associated with decentralization of career services. A highly decentralized system may include different department-specific software applications and vendors. At the extreme left end of the continuum (Figure 2.6), such

Figure 2.5. Career Information Resources Continuum.

Career Information Resource Systems

[_____]

Department-based information   Institution-wide career information
                                                via the career center

NEW DIRECTIONS FOR STUDENT SERVICES • DOI: 10.1002/ss

Figure 2.6. Recruiting and Other Software Systems Continuum.

Career Services Recruiting and Administrative Support Software Systems

[_____]

Varied department-based   Single integrated institution-wide

models are not very seamless, are not cost effective, and present different systems to employers and students within the same institution. Highly centralized institutions, falling to the extreme right of the dimension, offer a single institution-wide career services software system to students and employers.

Many institutions will fall in the middle range of the continuum. For example, some schools have various departments offering career programs using the same vendor but, in order to maintain departmental control, each career office purchases a separate software license. In this scenario, students may need to upload résumés in separate databases and employers may be required to post job/internship opportunities in separate systems within the same institution.

Some career services management systems allow institutions to purchase a shared system. Such "multi-school environment" systems allow offices that provide separate services and operate independently from each other to share some common data (e.g., students and employers) but retain independent customization and branding. This type of system allows each partner to share jobs, employers and contacts, and events and dual-affiliated students (i.e., students who work with both offices) all at significant potential cost savings and representing a more seamless institutional system (Hoover, Lenz, & Garis, 2013).

Ideally, even if separate career program recruiting software systems are in use within the same institution, the career center should take the lead to ensure that the institution-wide system in place is seamless for students and employers alike.

Many department- or college-based career programs begin with the mission to offer internship opportunities. Obviously, this is due to the academic linkages with internship programs. As a result, internship programs can easily become highly decentralized with minimal involvement with a central career services office. However, many internship opportunities are available to multiple majors, although some do not involve credit. Additionally, many academic department-based internship offices may use separate software systems requiring students and employers to post positions and/or résumés at multiple sites within the same institution. Acquiring institution-wide internship activity data can also present challenges in such colleges and universities. Even in highly decentralized internship programs, the career services office can take the lead in creating a website that serves as a portal for students and employers that includes all of the existing available internship programs. Such web-based applications are frequently referred to as *internship central or internship headquarters sites*. While politically far more challenging, the career services office can recommend one college/university software system to support all internship programs. Such software systems can be designed to allow for department-specific identity and control but offer the following advantages:

1. Only a single institutional software license is needed rather than costly and confusing multiple licenses.
2. Employers need to interact with only one software system when choosing to post internships.
3. Students can post the same résumé and need not register for multiple systems.
4. Collection of institution-wide internship data is available through a single software system.

At some schools, the central career center pays for the recruiting software license and trains the college partners to be able to use and tailor the system for their needs. Thus, the career center does the administrative support work with the involvement of college partners for decisions and design.

Of course, the same decentralization dynamics often applies to full-time employment programs. As many universities become more decentralized, it is common for schools to have multiple career fairs and events sponsored by departments, student organizations, colleges, and career services. In addition to career days, the mission of specialized college-based career offices may include career counseling, résumé reviews, mock interviewing, and/or on-campus interviewing. Also, colleges/department-based career programs may also use different software systems or hold individual licenses with the same software provider. Such decentralized practices can create a "silo model" for career services that is confusing to students and employers. In such institutions, the career services office can lead in creating a *landing page website* similar to the example noted earlier. The website does not change any departmental practices or control but offers a portal for students and employers to view the range of existing career and recruiting programs available at the institution. Also, as noted earlier, through the career center leadership, an institution can choose to adopt a hybrid recruiting model that includes the advantages of academic department/college-based career programs coupled with a strong institution-wide career services office. Such a model can be supported through a single recruiting system license that also allows for department/college-based identity and control. Regardless of the actual design, the career services office will add value to the institution by leading in proactively creating a career program and

Figure 2.7. Employer Relations Continuum.

Employer Relations Systems

[_____]

No career center involvement in   Employer relations led via
the institutional employer relations   the career center
program

recruiting a system model that is endorsed university-wide and is understood by students and employers.

Employer Relations Systems.   It would not be common to find career centers at the extremes of either side of the continuum in Figure 2.7. By nature, almost all career centers will be involved in employer relations but often other units such as an institution's corporate relations office will coordinate the college/university employer relations program. However, there are tremendous opportunities for career services to support employer relations systems falling in the continuum's center. Clearly, for example, career centers should lead in providing the institution with data including its school's top employers regarding recruiting and hiring activity. Also, the career center should be involved in employer development programs including employer visits that support corporate fundraising as well as employer support and sponsorship of research activities. Career center advisory boards frequently include employer members and can add to the college/university employer relations system. In supporting an institution-wide employer relations system, the career center will partner with the office of corporate relations, academic colleges, development offices, and in some cases student organizations.

Engaged Student Learning Programs and Systems.   In recent years, new engaged learning programs have been created that offer additional opportunities for career centers to add value in supporting and/or coordinating highly visible institution-wide programs (Figure 2.8). Examples include ePortfolios, leadership, and student engagement programs. Clearly, all of these programs hold the potential to support student career development. At some universities, career centers have led in the creation of ePortfolios that enjoyed the support of academic programs and became part of the institutional culture. ePortfolio systems often include skills matrices where

Figure 2.8. Engaged Learning Programs Continuum.

Engaged Student Learning Programs and Systems

[_____]

No career center involvement in   Formal career center programs
student engagement within the institution   supporting student engagement

NEW DIRECTIONS FOR STUDENT SERVICES • DOI: 10.1002/ss

students can include evidence of academic learning outcomes and professionally relevant skills acquired though a range of experiences. The skills are typically customizable for the student and their respective academic programs. However, examples of core skills available to students in creating ePortfolios include:

- communication,
- creativity,
- critical thinking,
- leadership,
- life experience,
- research,
- social responsibility,
- teamwork,
- technical/scientific, and
- writing.

Experiences supporting skill development may include:

- courses,
- jobs/internships,
- service/volunteerism,
- activities/memberships, and
- interests/life experiences.

Also, career centers have supported or led other university-wide initiatives such as student success, leadership, or student engagement programs. For example, student engagement programs can be created and include the career center to promote and recognize student involvement and accomplishment in the following areas:

- leadership,
- internships,
- service,
- international experience, and
- research.

Career centers will not typically shoulder responsibility for all of these engagement areas but can assume a leadership role in the overall program while partnering with academic affairs including undergraduate research as well as other university offices associated with specific engagement areas including student success centers, community/civic education, and student leadership/activities offices. In doing so, the career services office clearly adds to their value-added identification throughout the institution. It should be noted that a national trend may be emerging as several universities are creating models integrating career centers and leadership programs.

NEW DIRECTIONS FOR STUDENT SERVICES • DOI: 10.1002/ss

in translating theory to practice (Kidd, Killeen, Jarvis, & Offer, 1994). With the exception of counselors who attended one of the few accredited "career counseling" programs, most career professionals are not receiving comprehensive theoretical and practical training in career counseling during their graduate programs. In fact, the programs accredited by the Council for Accreditation of Counseling and Related Educational Programs (CACREP, 2009) typically offer only one career counseling course. Individuals who come into career services from diverse fields such as student affairs, human resources, and industry often have little exposure or knowledge of career development theories or counseling skills. While career professionals can read about theories, knowing a career development theory and executing it effectively take training and practice. Practical career counseling experience connected to readings is invaluable (Lara, Kline, & Paulson, 2011).

A basic premise of ongoing career counseling training is that theory informs practice. Some staff may be more competent in implementing theory into practice and more interested in theory, in general, while others may not realize how they already incorporate theory into their work (Pickerell, 2013). One way to engage staff in training is to give counselors the opportunity to learn different theoretical perspectives that connect to their individual interests, styles, or personalities. Counselors can be encouraged to teach other staff or lead discussions around incorporating theory into practice. Such a strategy ensures a variety of presentation, teaching, and learning styles along with a range of theories to discuss. Typically the time spent in group sessions will be more effective if participants have a basic understanding of the topic beforehand. Reading a relevant article or book chapter, reviewing a new or updated web resource (such as Going Global or LinkedIn), or utilizing an assessment tool are all great ways to actively engage counselors in gaining knowledge and connecting it to practice.

Skill Development.   At the core of counseling is relationship building and helping skills. Career counselors must be able to build quick and effective relationships with any student who seeks career services. An estimated 30% of successful counseling can be attributed to the relationship, or working alliance, involving caring, acceptance, affirmation, and encouragement (Ivey, Ivey, & Zalaquett, 2009). Attending behaviors, including listening, visual (eye contact), vocal (tone/pace/rate of speech), verbal tracking, and body language, need to be practiced, not simply understood. Appropriate open questions encourage students to talk more freely and openly while closed questions provide more information and specifics. Practicing these skills increases their effectiveness for assisting students with self-exploration and career decision making.

Microcounseling skills such as encouraging, paraphrasing, summarizing, active listening, and observation skills are critical to establishing rapport with clients (Ivey et al., 2009). Yet, in the hustle and bustle of career centers, with staff members juggling functional responsibilities in addition to seeing career counseling appointments, attending behaviors and microcounseling skills sometimes can fall by the wayside. Counselors become busy with other responsibilities and often want to hurry up and "tell" or "advise" the student without developing the relationship. When counselors fail to effectively build rapport, students are more likely to disengage. Intentionally practicing relationship-building skills in ongoing training ensures that these skills are at the forefront of each student interaction for all staff irrespective of their role in the office.

Practice, Practice, and More Practice.   No one learned to ride a bike by attending a PowerPoint presentation on bike riding. Riding a bike takes practice in order to feel safe and comfortable. Counseling is similar. Everyone needs to observe, practice, receive and discuss feedback, and practice more. At the University of Illinois at Urbana-Champaign, several strategies are used to structure practice, encourage observation, and increase learning. While staff often cringes at the mention of practicing in front of others, keep in mind that training should be uncomfortable at times in order to promote growth. Sample case studies can provide opportunities to practice specific situations while also assisting the "clients" in playing their roles. Undergraduate student workers may be willing to serve as clients, either playing themselves or role-playing a case study. Some role-play activities are described next.

Small Group Role-Play.   This is the traditional three-person group in which two individuals role-play and the third observes and provides feedback. Small group role-play can be utilized early in training when participants may feel anxious. Each individual should play each of the three roles: client, counselor, and observer with time to debrief each session.

Popcorn Role-Play.   The "client" sits in the center of the room. Each counselor around the circle can ask one question only (sometimes one follow-up is allowed) or make one comment. The role-play continues until the counselors have effectively assisted the student and the appointment comes to a close. Afterward, the group processes the appointment: What questions were surprising? What questions were particularly helpful? What would people have done differently? Popcorn is a practical way to learn from each other's styles and strategies.

Tag Role-Play.   Tag is set up similarly to popcorn, except in this case, one counselor begins the counseling with the student client. The counselor continues to counsel the client until he or she gets stuck. Then the counselor "tags" someone else to continue the appointment, and the "new" counselor may use another strategy or approach. This process is repeated several times and highlights how differently each staff member may approach the student and their career concern.

Learning by Observation.   Research has shown that humans "learn" behaviors through observation (Bandura, 1977). Every accredited graduate counseling program includes a process for graduate students to observe professionals. Telling someone how to do career counseling is not enough; staff will learn and be able to implement new strategies more effectively if

Cambridge, D., Kaplan, S., & Suter, V. (2005). *Community of practice design guide*. Retrieved from http://net.educause.edu/ir/library/pdf/nli0531.pdf

Collegiate Employment Research Institute. (2014). *Recruiting trends 2013–2014* (43rd ed.). East Lansing, MI: Author. Retrieved from http://www.ceri.msu.edu/recruiting-trends/recruiting-trends-2013-2014/

Cosh, J. (1998). Peer observation in higher education—A reflective approach. *Innovations in Education and Teaching International, 35*(2), 171–176.

Council for Accreditation of Counseling and Related Educational Programs. (2009). *2009 standards*. Retrieved from http://www.cacrep.org/wp-content/uploads/2013/12/2009-Standards.pdf

Feltovich, P. J., Prietula, M. J., & Ericsson, K. A. (2006). Studies of expertise from psychological perspectives. In K. A. Ericsson, N. Charness, P. Feltovich, & R. R. Hoffman (Eds.), *Cambridge handbook of expertise and expert performance* (pp. 39–68). Cambridge, UK: Cambridge University Press.

Hartung, P. J. (2005). Internalizing career counseling: Emptying our cups and learning from each other. *The Career Development Quarterly, 54*, 12–16.

Heppner, M. I., & Johnston, J. A. (1993). Career counseling: A call for action. In J. R. Rayman (Ed.), *New Directions for Student Services: No. 62. The changing role of career services* (pp. 57–78). San Francisco, CA: Jossey-Bass.

Ivey, A. E., Ivey, M. B., & Zalaquett, C. P. (2009). *Intentional interviewing and counseling: Facilitating client development in a multicultural society* (7th ed.). Pacific Grove, CA: Brooks Cole.

Kidd, J., Killeen, J., Jarvis, J., & Offer, M. (1994). Is guidance an applied science? The role of theory in the careers guidance interview. *British Journal of Guidance and Counseling, 22*, 385–403.

Lara, T. M., Kline, W. B., & Paulson, D. (2011). Attitudes regarding career counseling perceptions and experiences of counselors-in-training. *Career Development Quarterly, 59*(5), 428–440.

Lave, J., & Wenger, E. (1991). *Situated learning: Legitimate peripheral participation*. Cambridge, MA: Cambridge University Press.

Makela, J. P. (2011). *Career counseling as an environmental support: Exploring influences on career choice, career decision-making self-efficacy, and career barriers* (Unpublished doctoral dissertation). University of Illinois at Urbana-Champaign, Champaign.

Makela, J. P., & Rooney, G. S. (2012). *Learning outcomes assessment step-by-step: Enhancing evidence-based practice in career services*. Broken Arrow, OK: National Career Development Association.

Martin, G. A., & Double, J. M. (1998). Developing higher education teaching skills through peer observation and collaborative reflection. *Innovations in Education and Teaching International, 35*(2), 161–170.

Meister, J. (2012, August 14). Job hopping is the new normal for Millennials: Three ways to prevent a human resource nightmare. *Forbes.com*. Retrieved from http://www.forbes.com/sites/jeannemeister/2012/08/14/job-hopping-is-the-new-normal-for-millennials-three-ways-to-prevent-a-human-resource-nightmare/

National Association of Colleges and Employers (NACE). (2012, July). *Position statement: The critical importance of institutional first-destination/post-graduation surveys*. Retrieved from http://www.naceweb.org/advocacy/position-statements/first-destination-surveys.aspx

National Association of Colleges and Employers (NACE). (2014). *NACE 2013–2014 career services benchmark survey for colleges and universities*. Bethlehem, PA: Author.

National Career Development Association (NCDA). (2009). *Minimum competencies for multicultural career counseling and development*. Broken Arrow, OK: Author. Retrieved from http://www.associationdatabase.com/aws/NCDA/asset_manager/get_file/9914/minimum_competencies_for_multi-cultural_career_counseling.pdf?ver=5617

Niles, S. G. (2013). Career counseling. In M. L. Savickas (Ed.), *Ten ideas that changed career development: A monograph to celebrate the centennial of the National Career Development Association (1913–2013)* (p. 4). Broken Arrow, OK: National Career Development Association.

Orbé-Austin, R. (2010, April). Multicultural career counseling competence: 5 key tips for improving practice. *Career Convergence.* Broken Arrow, OK: National Career Development Association. Retrieved from http://ncda.org/aws/NCDA/pt/sd/news_article/28865/_self/layout_details/false

Patterson, K., Grenny, J., Maxfield, D., McMillian, R., & Switzler, A. (2008). *Influencer: The power to change anything.* New York, NY: McGraw-Hill.

Pickerell, D. A. (2013). When did you last think about theory. *Career Convergence.* Broken Arrow, OK: National Career Development Association. Retrieved from http://www.ncda.org/aws/NCDA/pt/sd/news_article/82014/_PARENT/layout_details_cc/false

Rath, T., & Harter, J. (2010). *Wellbeing: The five essential elements.* New York, NY: Gallup Press.

Rayman, J. R. (Ed.). (1993). *New Directions for Student Services: No. 62. The changing role of career services.* San Francisco, CA: Jossey-Bass.

Sampson, J. P., Dozier, V. C., & Colvin, G. P. (2011). Translating career theory to practice: The risk of unintentional social justice. *Journal of Counseling and Development, 89*(3), 326–337.

Savickas, M. L. (2011). Constructing careers: Actor, agent, and author. *Journal of Employment Counseling, 48*(4), 179–181.

Savickas, M. L. (Ed.). (2013). *Ten ideas that changed career development: A monograph to celebrate the centennial of the National Career Development Association (1913–2013).* Broken Arrow, OK: National Career Development Association.

Shortland, S. (2010). Feedback within peer observations: Continuing professional development and unexpected consequences. *Innovations in Education and Teaching International, 47*(3), 295–304.

Sue, D. W., Capodilupo, C. M., Torino, G. C., Bucceri, J. M., Holder, A. M., Nadal, K. L., & Esquilin, M. (2007). Racial microaggressions in everyday life: Implications for clinical practice. *American Psychologist, 62*(4), 271–286.

Sue, D. W., & Sue, D. (2003). *Counseling the culturally diverse: Theory and practice* (4th ed.). Hoboken, NJ: Wiley.

Wenger, E., McDermott, R., & Snyder, W. (2002). *Cultivating communities of practice: A guide to managing knowledge.* Boston, MA: Harvard School Press.

Wenger-Trayner, E. (n.d.). *Communities of practice: A brief introduction.* Retrieved from http://wenger-trayner.com/theory/

The White House. (2013, August 22). *Fact sheet on the President's plan to make college more affordable: A better bargain for the middle class* [Press Release]. Retrieved from http://www.whitehouse.gov/the-press-office/2013/08/22/fact-sheet-president-s-plan-make-college-more-affordable-better-bargain-

KERI CARTER PIPKINS is an associate director at The Career Center, University of Illinois at Urbana-Champaign.

GAIL S. ROONEY is an associate dean of Leadership and Career Development, University of Illinois at Urbana-Champaign.

IMANTS JAUNARAJS is an assistant dean of students at Career and Leadership Development Center, Ohio University.

This chapter describes how career services professionals and academic advising units can partner to serve college students. Observations are also provided regarding the role of advising and best practices to meet the growing need for a shared approach to the academic and career needs of students.

Academic Advising and Career Services: A Collaborative Approach

Katherine E. Ledwith

The economy and state and federal government policies, along with input from parents, employers, and other stakeholders, are some of the factors creating an increased focus on career services at colleges and universities. In August 2013, President Obama submitted a proposal to link federal financial aid programs to a standardized college rating system based on factors including student completion rates and graduate earnings by the year 2015 (Fain, 2013; Office of the White House Press Secretary, 2013). As higher education officials are asked to provide more data on student graduation rates and subsequent career paths, the need for a more collaborative partnership between academic advising and career services for college students grows.

As many academic advising and career services professionals point out (Bullock, Reardon, & Lenz, 2007; Gordon, 2006; Hughey & Hughey, 2009; Lenz, McCaig, & Carr, 2010), the need to better integrate elements of career and academic advising is not a new one. They note the increasing number of specialized and practical arts degree programs, work options, and in some cases the "mission creep" of academic advising services as factors that have provided an impetus for greater collaboration. Given recent external pressures, some higher education professionals are increasingly advocating for a change in how career services offices operate in relation to other academic units (Rethinking Success Conference, 2013). As institutions call for academic offices to provide support, assistance, and accountability with regard to students' postgraduate career outcomes, it is important that career services professionals be proactive in their efforts to work together with academic advising counterparts.

This chapter will focus on collaborative, adaptive methods as cost-effective solutions within the context of existing career and academic advising structures. This chapter comments briefly on historical precedent;

New Directions for Student Services, no. 148, Winter 2014 © 2014 Wiley Periodicals, Inc.
Published online in Wiley Online Library (wileyonlinelibrary.com) • DOI: 10.1002/ss.20108

highlights career and academic advising similarities and differences; proposes ideas for establishing a partnership that include shared publications, programming, marketing, evaluation, and assessment; and presents conclusions related to the value of a partnered approach to academic and career advising for students.

Historical Origins of Advising

Historically, academic advising and career services share a common functional origin point as both offices arose on higher education campuses out of a need to advise students on important information. Academic advising started in the colonial times with college administration and faculty sharing curricular information (Gordon, 2006). Today, academic advising is accomplished by a variety of faculty, professionals, and paraprofessionals, often within more than one organizational structure on a particular higher education campus (National Academic Advising Association, 2011). Several authors (Herr, Rayman, & Garis, 1993; Hoover, Lenz, & Garis, 2013) discuss the evolution of career centers from placement offices, that is, places of advising on employment leads and alumni contacts, to more comprehensive service delivery models that include career counseling and assessment to all class levels. Today's career centers can include services ranging from career fairs, workshops, internship, co-op, and externship opportunities to career resources and assessment, drop-in career advising, and career counseling by appointment (National Association of Colleges and Employers, 2014).

Advising Today

Today, both career and academic offices offer advising services that overlap in key ways. Career centers typically offer career advising and/or career counseling. Many authors (Bullock et al., 2007; Gordon, 2006; Herr et al., 1993; Hughey & Hughey, 2009; Niles & Harris-Bowlsbey, 2012) offer thoughts on defining career counseling and career advising as well the similarities and differences between them. Career counseling "involves a formal relationship in which a professional counselor assists a client, or a group of clients, to cope more effectively with career concerns (e.g., making a career choice, coping with career transitions, coping with job-related stress, or job searching)" (Niles & Harris-Bowlsbey, 2012, p. 16). Gordon (2006) notes that career counseling differs from career advising as being more psychological and problem focused and defines career advising as a process "which helps student[s] understand how their personal interests, abilities, and values might predict success in the academic and career fields they are considering and how to form their academic and career goals accordingly" (p. 12). Career advising, as delineated here, encompasses both career and academic aspects. For example, career advisors might discuss occupational options as related to institutional majors, as well as professional and graduate school options. Career advising may be performed by a variety of career services practitioners including career advisors, career counselors, and many other types of career development professionals.

Several articles discuss the foundations of career advising and its relation to academic advising (Gordon, 2006; Hughey & Hughey, 2009; Nelson & McCalla-Wriggins, 2009). According to the National Academic Advising Association (2006), academic advising "synthesizes and conceptualizes students' educational experiences within the frameworks of their aspirations, abilities and lives to extend learning beyond campus boundaries and timeframes" (p. 2). Hughey and Hughey (2009) noted that a "learning-centered approach facilitates career and academic advising and contributes to student learning relative to academic, career, and personal goals" (p. 5). The basic definition of academic advising includes career elements, and there has been a movement to further integrate career factors into academic advising (Gordon, 2006). The traditional idea of primarily academic-focused advising is changing. Academic advisors play a key role in providing education options as related to students' career goals, and how their decisions may impact future career paths. In this functional way, academic and career services practitioners share the common goal of assisting students with career concerns within an educational framework.

Current Contextual View of Collaboration

Creamer, Creamer, and Brown (2003) noted that academic advising interacts with all academic departments, as well as student services, and "offers a unique site for collaboration, which is essential to achieve [institutional] excellence" (p. 205). While a shared focus on student goals links career and academic units, collaboration between academic advising and career services units varies wide in practice. Bullock et al. (2007) noted that a variety of approaches appear to work well and provide several model examples of academic advising and career services collaboration. Nelson and McCalla-Wriggins (2009) discussed the advantages and disadvantages of formal and informal approaches to career and academic advising office integration. Current information on career center and advising amalgamation highlights potential factors influencing this wide range of collaboration.

Institutional Type. Because career centers vary widely in their mission, focus, funding, size, and, consequently, services offered, some offices have an existing functional overlap with academic advising. A proportionally small number of career services offices (24.7%) provide academic "counseling," primarily at schools with multipurpose units (National Association of Colleges and Employers, 2014). The highest number of respondents (60%) who reported academic counseling available at their career center were those from associate's degree colleges. Bullock et al. (2007) noted the NACADA website lists offices with both career and academic offerings have names such as "Advising and Career Services," "Center for Academic and Career Development," and the "Center for Advising and Career Services" (National Academic Advising Association, 2013).

Reporting Lines.   The reporting structure of a career center may affect the extent to which a career services unit might partner with an academic advising office (Herr et al., 1993). For example, a career center housed in and reporting to a counseling center could potentially have a greater counseling, rather than advising, approach to the career development process. The 2013–2014 NACE Career Services Benchmark Survey for Four-Year Colleges and Universities found that of 840 university career offices surveyed, 18.9% fell under the organizational division of "Academic Affairs," contrasted with 59.0% who fell under "Student Affairs." Because most career centers are not housed under their institution's academic unit, career services and academic professionals in these settings may need to more intentionally reach out to their university counterparts. In addition, considerations regarding funding mutual career interventions may need to be made in light of two separately budgeted units.

Organizational Structure.   A career center's collaboration with external constituents may also be affected by its centralized or decentralized organizational structure (Herr et al., 1993; Hoover et al., 2013). A survey of 866 career services offices found that 84.2% were centralized (National Association of Colleges and Employers, 2014). With growing demands for accountability from academic units to document graduate success following program completion, some institutions have seen an increase in academic units looking to create satellite career offices or requesting major-focused career services. In turn, this places increased pressure on career services units to not only provide generalized services to any population, but also to work with academic units to meet the unique needs of many campus subpopulations.

Foundations of Collaborative Success

Given the current need for more collaborative efforts between academic advising and career services units, many career services practitioners are increasing their role in working with academic advising colleagues. It can be worthwhile for career practitioners to complete several initial action steps prior to codeveloping any career interventions. Taking time to identify the correct staff and conferring with them regarding considerations related to student readiness for career decision making and specific functional roles increase the odds of collaborating effectively.

Examine Advising Structure.   The 2011 NACADA National Survey reports that no specific advising model is used at a majority of institutions, but rather that the model was related to the size of the organization. For example, most large institutions (greater than 24,000 students) utilize a "self-contained" model, where academic advisors are professional staff housed in

discussed academic and career services copresenting a "majors and careers" fair. Reaching out to academic units to include them on career center events fosters a win–win situation for students because they receive targeted academic and career information. Collaborative programming also provides an opportunity for career advisors-in-training (such as graduate students in a career counseling program) to learn about the process of working with other departmental units, and to polish their external relations, public speaking, and event planning skills. For example, career staff can partner with an academic advisor to plan and copresent a workshop for exploratory students.

Resources.   Designing and developing resources with academic advisors can range from print materials such as "Match Major to Occupations" sheets to electronic materials such as shared links on advising program maps to career center resources. For some campuses, it is not clear to students how to delineate the differences between academic advisors and career advisors, and such materials can be helpful in distinguishing their services. When worked on together, print materials can also reflect the collaborative relationship between the two entities. The same can be true for electronic promotional materials and departmental websites.

Case Study: Partnering for Exploratory Students

Special student populations such as exploratory students, first-generation college students, athletes, transfer students, veterans, limited access majors, or international students can be an excellent starting place for career and academic advisors to work collaboratively. Provided next is a case study of how career services professionals and academic advisors at one large, research-based public institution utilized the tools above to support exploratory and undecided students.

Background.   Exploratory and undecided students comprise a student population that lends itself well for academic and career collaboration. With staff cuts and shrinking budgets at some institutions, it is often difficult to provide excellent student-focused services for time-intensive exploratory student populations. Although career services professionals and academic advising units have different functional goals, these offices can collaborate to assist students undecided about their majors. The FSU Career Center in partnership with FSU's Advising First Center for Exploratory Students provides interactive programming through a series of workshops and events held regularly throughout the year. While targeted toward students undecided about their major, these events are open and widely attended by students from all majors.

Workshops.   Each semester, the FSU Career Center and the Center for Exploratory Students jointly sponsor six "Pizza and a Major" workshops for 400 or more students. These interactive workshops provided exploratory students with high-quality, individualized assistance and an orientation to Career Center services. The purpose of the workshops is to help students select an appropriate major by exposing them to strategies for gaining self-knowledge, and resources for exploring majors and occupations.

Student Conferences.   Career and academic advising staff have also developed and implemented an annual Student Success Conference that targets freshmen and exploratory students. The conference differed from the workshops by its broader focus and drop-in format. At Florida State University in 2012, over 300 students attended six featured sessions and spoke with representatives from 25 different on-campus departments and organizations to learn how they can succeed at the university.

Panels.   Each spring, the two offices organize and host a series of "Exploratory Panels" for six different academic areas featuring professionals working in or having specialized knowledge of various professional fields. The panels include faculty, staff, and students who share general information, advice, and personal success stories to help inform students about their department/major. The panels are offered as an extra credit activity in the career development class taught by career center staff.

Tools.   Staff members from the FSU Career Center and Exploratory Advising created the "Choosing a Major or Occupation Guide," which contains a series of activities an exploratory student can complete with the assistance of academic and career advisors. The guide is a unique collaborative tool that is cocreated, revised, and utilized by both the Career Center and the Center for Exploratory Students. An exploratory student is referred easily between departments, and the guide prevents duplication of services while allowing the expertise of both units to be fully utilized.

As noted above, for some student populations, academic advising and career advising shared interventions may look very different from a traditional one-on-one meeting format. For example, many graduate students receive advice regarding their course of study from their major professor and/or program coordinator who serve as their de facto academic advisors. In this instance, career services professionals may need to target graduate faculty to assisting this student population. At Florida State University, career center staff assisted the graduate school in creating a "Preparing Future Professionals" program open to all graduate school students. By participating in a specific number of workshops on career-related topics, graduate students can earn a certificate and thus combine the flexibility of their degree program with valuable career information. It is important to think creatively, openly, and broadly about the best ways to meet the career needs for special population students and in relation to their individual academic paths.

Summary

There is an increasing need for career advising to be an integral part of the academic advising experience. Career services professionals and academic

NEW DIRECTIONS FOR STUDENT SERVICES • DOI: 10.1002/ss

advising units can use their shared functional roles and goals of student success as a basis for working together. While it is important to work within areas of expertise, it is helpful for each "subject expert" (career or academic) to team up with the other to combine their knowledge and skill sets. Prior consideration of foundational elements such as organization structures, students' readiness, and individual roles can be beneficial. For career advising and academic advising practitioners, clear communication targeting key staff members, referrals, and cross-training can aid in the development and ongoing success of shared programming and resources.

Data collection and self-assessment allow for ongoing formative and summative evaluation of these services. Just over half (56.5%) of the career services offices surveyed had conducted self-assessment in the past five years (National Association of Colleges and Employers, 2014). Lenz et al. (2010) offer several general self-review questions for career and academic offices engaged in collaboration. Both formal and informal evaluation can be prepared for distribution to major and degree programs, and shared with academic departments, staff, and administration. Wider distribution and best practices in collaborative efforts can be accomplished by presenting jointly at professional conferences and meetings. Additional methods for career and academic advisors to grow in their knowledge and understanding to benefit collaborative work might include:

- Reading resources to assist in understanding each other's viewpoint and techniques (e.g., industry publications or professional journals such as the *NACADA Journal* or the *Journal of Career Development* to learn more about academic or career advising).
- Participating in joint webinars, conferences, meetings, professional associations, and committees.
- Completing self-assessment activities to identify areas of growth such as Virginia Gordon's "What Is Your Career Advising IQ?" for academic advisors (Gordon, 2005).

These activities are just a few among many possible proactive learning activities for career and academic advising staff. It is crucial for career practitioners and academic advisors to think critically about their professional development to help college students develop a personal integrated academic and career plan. Career services professionals play a vital role in reaching out to, building relationships with, and collaborating with academic advising personnel. With time and money in short supply, and the growing pressure for more timely completion of college degrees, the need for career and academic collaboration has never been greater. To provide students with the best possible services, career and advising offices need to intentionally partner with each other. By actively working together, career and academic units can support the career developmental needs of today's college students.

References

Bullock, E. E., Reardon, R. C., & Lenz, J. G. (2007). Planning good academic and career decisions. In G. L. Kramer & Associates (Eds.), *Fostering student success in the campus community* (pp. 193–213). San Francisco, CA: Jossey-Bass.

Carr, D. L., & Epstein, S. A. (2009). Information resources to enhance career advising. In K. F. Hughey, D. Nelson, J. K. Damminger, & B. McCalla-Wriggins (Eds.), *The handbook of career advising* (1st ed., pp. 146–181). San Francisco, CA: Jossey-Bass.

Chickering, A. W., & Reisser, L. (1993). *Education and identity* (2nd ed.). San Francisco, CA: Jossey-Bass.

Creamer, D. G., & Creamer, E. G. (1994). Practicing developmental advising: Theoretical contexts and functional applications. *NACADA Journal, 14*(2), 17–24.

Creamer, E. G., Creamer, D. G., & Brown, K. S. (2003). Applying quality educational principles to academic advising. In G. L. Kramer & E. D. Peterson (Eds.), *Student academic services in higher education: A comprehensive handbook for the 21st century* (pp. 205–222). San Francisco, CA: Jossey-Bass.

Fain, P. (2013, August 23). Performance funding goes federal. *Inside Higher Education.* Retrieved from http://www.insidehighered.com/news/2013/08/23/higher-education-leaders-respond-obamas-ambitous-ratings-system-plan

Gordon, V. N. (2005). What is your career advising IQ? *Academic Advising Today, 28*(4). Retrieved from http://www.nacada.ksu.edu/Resources/Academic-Advising-Today/View-Articles/What-is-Your-Career-Advising-IQ.aspx

Gordon, V. N. (2006). *Career advising: An academic advisor's guide.* San Francisco, CA: Jossey-Bass.

Herr, E. L., Rayman, J. R., & Garis, J. W. (1993). *Handbook for the college and university career center.* Westport, CT: Greenwood Publishing Group.

Hoover, M. P., Lenz, J. G., & Garis, J. W. (2013). *Employer relations and recruitment: An essential part of postsecondary career services.* Broken Arrow, OK: National Career Development Association.

Hughey, K. F., & Hughey, J. K. (2009). Foundations of career advising. In. K. F. Hughey & National Academic Advising Association (Eds.), *The handbook of career advising* (pp. 1–18). San Francisco, CA: Jossey-Bass.

Lenz, J. G., McCaig, K. A., & Carr, D. L. (2010). Career services and academic advising: Collaborating for student success. *NACE Journal, 71*(2), 30–35.

National Academic Advising Association. (2006). *NACADA concept of academic advising.* Retrieved from http://www.nacada.ksu.edu/Resources/Clearinghouse/View-Articles/Concept-of-Academic-Advising-a598.aspx

National Academic Advising Association. (2011). *NACADA national survey of academic advising.* Retrieved from http://www.nacada.ksu.edu/Resources/Clearinghouse/View-Articles/2011-NACADA-National-Survey.aspx

National Academic Advising Association. (2013). *Career advising centers.* Retrieved from http://www.nacada.ksu.edu/Resources/Clearinghouse/View-Articles/Career-advising-centers.aspx

National Association of Colleges and Employers. (2014). *NACE 2013–2014 career services benchmark survey for four-year colleges and universities.* Bethlehem, PA: Author.

Nelson, D. B., & McCalla-Wriggins, B. (2009). Integrated career and academic advising programs. In K. F. Hughey & National Academic Advising Association (Eds.), *The handbook of career advising* (pp. 200–216). San Francisco, CA: Jossey-Bass.

Niles, S. G., & Harris-Bowlsbey, J. A. (2012). *Career development interventions in the 21st century.* Upper Saddle River, NJ: Merrill/Pearson.

Office of the White House Press Secretary. (2013). Fact sheet on the President's plan to make college more affordable: A better bargain for the middle class. *Office of the White House.* Retrieved from http://www.whitehouse.gov/the-press-office/2013/08/22/fact-sheet-president-s-plan-make-college-more-affordable-better-bargain-

Peterson, G. W., Lenz, J. G., & Sampson, J. P. (2003). The assessment of readiness for student learning in college. In G. L. Kramer & Associates (Eds.), *Student academic services: An integrated approach* (pp. 103–125). San Francisco, CA: Jossey-Bass.

Reardon, R. C., Folsom, B., Lee, D., & Clark, J. (2011, July 11). *The effects of college career courses on learner outputs and outcomes* (Tech. Rep. 53). Tallahassee: Center for the Study of Technology in Counseling & Career Development, Florida State University. Retrieved from http://www.career.fsu.edu/techcenter/whatsnew/TechRept53.pdf

Rethinking Success Conference. (2013). *A roadmap for transforming the college-to-career experience: A crowdsourced paper* [White paper]. Retrieved from http://rethinkingsuccess.wfu.edu/files/2013/05/A-Roadmap-for-Transforming-The-College-to-Career-Experience.pdf

Sampson, J. P. (2008). *Designing and implementing career programs: A handbook for effective practice.* Broken Arrow, OK: National Career Development Association.

Sampson, J. P., Reardon, R. C., Peterson, G. W., & Lenz, J. G. (2004). *Career counseling and services: A cognitive information processing approach.* Belmont, CA: Thomson/Brooks/Cole.

KATHERINE E. LEDWITH is a coordinator of Pathway Advising at Pikes Peak Community College.

Appendix A: Sample Liaison Activities

Sample activities that might be part of the peer career advisor liaison role include the following:

- Making recommendations regarding career information and/or job search resources that should be maintained by the career center to meet the specific needs of students in the various academic programs of the college.
- Making sure the school/college gets copies of career center materials (e.g., career guides, bookmarks, etc.; publicity flyers for futures, etc.), especially keeping any peer advising office stocked with materials.
- Faxing or emailing job notices received by the career center to key staff that might be of interest to students in a particular school/college.
- Becoming familiar with the career/academic needs of students enrolled in specific majors within the college and inform/train other career advisors regarding this information.
- Developing selected materials, services, or programs (career forums, workshops) to help students identify the range of career alternatives and job opportunities associated with majors in that college. This could also include revising and updating previously existing career center materials (e.g., match major sheets) and resources related to a particular discipline.
- Developing links between the career center and college websites that address career information and services specific to the college and its majors.
- Recommending website links that relate to the needs of students in a particular college/school.
- Attending meetings of academic advisors/faculty and providing the career center with current information associated with their respective college and informing the college/school of current career center services.
- Inviting advisors and other staff from the school/college to a career center open house.
- Generally serving as a contact and conduit for the exchange of information and referrals between the respective college and the career center.
- Meeting individually with students from a particular school/college who need more in-depth assistance with their career planning and/or job hunting.
- Others as appropriate.

Appendix B: Top Ten Ways

The top 10 career center resources for academic advisors to use in helping students explore options and increase their career success:

1. Encourage students to use key occupational information and computer-based guidance sites, such as ONET, OOH, CHOICES: http://www.career.fsu.edu/occupations/exploring_occupations.cfm

2. Use the career center's "matching majors with job information sheets" to expand students' knowledge of opportunities and work settings related to their field of study: http://www.career.fsu.edu/occupations/matchmajor/

3. Remind students to obtain SeminolePlus! services to learn more about the job opportunities employers are offering and to access on-line resources such as CareerShift and Going Global.

4. Encourage students to enroll in the SDS 3340 Introduction to Career Development class to engage in more in-depth career exploration and preparation: http://www.career.fsu.edu/courses/sds3340/

5. Invite students to access ProfessioNole to learn more about the career paths of FSU alumni and friends: http://career.fsu.edu/professionole/

6. Use FSU's Career Portfolio to show students how they can high-light their skills and samples of their work to prospective employers: https://apps.oti.fsu.edu/CareerPortfolio/jsp/login.jsp

7. Promote FSU Career Center events that will help students in making career decisions and interacting with prospective employers: http://career.fsu.edu/calendar/

8. Encourage students to use the career center's in-depth career library resources, both print and online, to expand their knowledge of options: http://www.career.fsu.edu/library/

9. Promote internship opportunities in SeminoleLink as a way of exploring career options and gaining valuable experience: http://www.career.fsu.edu/internships_and_co-ops/

10. Refer students to drop-in career advising for help in developing an individual career plan related to their educational and employment goals: http://www.career.fsu.edu

5

This chapter provides career professionals with an overview of current assessment practices and a framework for understanding how to bring practitioner-led assessment activities into daily practice.

Framing Assessment for Career Services: Telling Our Story

Julia Panke Makela, Gail S. Rooney

What is the value of career services? What difference do career services make in students' lives? How do we know? Articulating compelling responses to these questions is essential for career development professionals to advocate for the work that they do. Engaging in assessment is a powerful tool to help career professionals "tell the story" of their programs, services, and resources, as well as the students that they reach (Makela & Rooney, 2012; Shulman, 2007). Assessment offers opportunities to gather evidence to enhance career development work through a process of continuous improvement as well as highlighting the importance of the functions that career professionals serve in interactions with multiple stakeholders.

Recognizing the need for assessment is not necessarily new to career professionals. We have long engaged in efforts to understand student needs, track participation, and measure satisfaction—types of assessments that characterize the programs, services, and resources that are offered to students by career services offices. However, the types of assessment data desired by stakeholders have evolved and expanded over time (Schuh & Gansemer-Topf, 2010). In more recent years, career professionals have been asked to demonstrate the results of participating in career interventions—how students have changed or what they gain from participation. The impetus for this new focus in assessment efforts has come from the broader campus environment that faces persistent calls from external constituents (e.g., accrediting associations, governments, students, and families) who want to know that they will receive a "good return on their own and society's educational investment" (Guskin, 1994, p. 22) in higher education. For example, see *An American Imperative: Higher Expectations for Higher Education* (Wingspread Group on Higher Education, 1993), *A Test of Leadership: Charting the Future of American Higher Education* (U.S. Department

New Directions for Student Services, no. 148, Winter 2014 © 2014 Wiley Periodicals, Inc.
Published online in Wiley Online Library (wileyonlinelibrary.com) • DOI: 10.1002/ss.20109

of Education, 2006; also known as *The Spellings Commission Report*), and *The College Scorecard* initiative (The White House, 2013). When career professionals use assessment efforts to demonstrate knowledge gained by students who participate in career interventions, they build a strong narrative to advocate for the unique ways that career services contributes to higher education environments. Career services can demonstrate alignment with the central education mission of colleges and universities, and encourage collaborations with academic departments and administrators who are also seeking to demonstrate student learning and development (Makela & Rooney, 2012).

The purpose of this chapter is to provide career professionals with an overview of current assessment practices in career services, as well as a framework for understanding how to bring practitioner-led assessment activities into daily practice. The chapter begins with a definition of assessment, including illustrations of the key elements of that definition and distinctions made between assessment of career interventions and other related activities. A rationale is presented encouraging career professionals to engage in assessment both for continuous improvement and to demonstrate the value of programs, services, and resources. Various types of assessment are introduced and defined, including needs, participation, satisfaction, and outcomes, with brief discussions of the value of each approach. The chapter concludes with a discussion of strategies for motivating assessment activities within career services offices as well as suggested resources for getting started.

Framing Assessment for Career Interventions

Career interventions refer to the programs, services, and resources offered by career professionals to help students explore career options and make career choices, as well as define, implement, and manage career plans. The term "assessment" has historically been used broadly, with many meanings that vary across different fields of practice (Suskie, 2009; Wehlburg, 2008). Therefore, we frame our discussion of assessment by defining key elements of the assessment process. Distinctions are then made between assessment and other related activities familiar to career professionals, including research and evaluation.

Elements of Assessment. We define assessment as "a continuous process of gathering and interpreting evidence to tell a story about the effectiveness of career interventions for the dual purposes of continuous improvement and celebrating successes" (Makela & Rooney, 2012, p. 1). Consider each of the elements in this definition.

Continuous Process. While early views of assessment primarily focus on collection of data at the end of a program or service, contemporary views of assessment take a more integrated approach (e.g., Makela

& Rooney, 2012; Suskie, 2009). Assessment is a continuous process that includes (a) defining context and desired outcomes for a career intervention, (b) determining what type of evidence can demonstrate whether or not desired outcomes are achieved, (c) delivering the career intervention, (d) gathering and analyzing data, (e) interpreting data, (f) using the findings, (g) returning to redefine context and desired outcomes, and (h) beginning the cycle anew. As such, assessment permeates every stage of designing, delivering, and improving career interventions.

Gathering and Interpreting Evidence. The collection and interpretation of evidence is of central importance to assessment, surrounded by an ongoing process that incorporates interpreting data, communicating findings for multiple audiences and purposes, and using findings to improve practice. Evidence is the data used to make a persuasive argument regarding what aspects of career interventions work well and what aspects can be improved.

This can be quite challenging, as many types of evidence exist (e.g., participation numbers, expression of satisfaction, and learning outcomes) and can be measured in many ways (e.g., surveys, focus groups, and portfolios). Career professionals must first determine what data will inform their practice and provide persuasive arguments to their target audiences. Then, evidence needs to be collected in a planned and systematic manner, so that the quality of the evidence can be defended. Finally, the data that are gathered do not speak for themselves. Career professionals and other key stakeholders (such as administrators, students, and employers) must analyze and interpret data to improve career interventions based on evidence rather than anecdotes or hunches.

Tells a Story. Assessment is essentially a process of telling a story about people, programs, services, and resources (Shulman, 2007). There are many possible stories to tell and many ways of telling those stories. Just like writing a good novel, we make decisions along the way. What story do we want to tell? What audiences (or stakeholders) are we creating this story for? What story lines (or evidence) will be highlighted? What will be left out? The storyline surrounding an assessment ultimately aims to include enough evidence to make well-reasoned assertions about the effectiveness of career interventions and motivate career professionals, students, and other stakeholders to take action (Suskie, 2009; Swing & Coogan, 2010).

Dual Purposes of Improvement and Accountability. The "assessment movement" (Ewell, 2009, p. 5) in U.S. higher education began in the early 1980s with a sense of tension between two dual purposes: accountability and improvement. Assessment for accountability relates to pressures and demands, often from external stakeholders, to demonstrate the "importance and worth" (Upcraft & Schuh, 1996, p. 9) of career interventions in an environment of increased competition for limited and declining resources. How can we know a particular career intervention makes a difference, is necessary, or is cost effective? As such, accountability provides an "incentive for [an] entity to look as good as possible, regardless of the underlying performance" (Ewell, 2009, p. 7). As a result, accountability efforts often limit discussions of assessment to what went well. Assessment for improvement, on the other hand, often stems from internal stakeholders and relates to desires to enhance the quality of a program or service. The goal of improvement requires assessments to actively seek, uncover, and report performance deficiencies so that appropriate actions may be taken (Ewell, 2009).

Attempting to serve the dual purposes of accountability and improvement may seem fundamentally at odds. Rather than juxtaposing these two purposes as opposites, we find it more productive to consider them as endpoints on a continuum. Assessment efforts rarely fall at the extremes, serving only accountability or only improvement (Ewell, 2009). Rather, it is desirable to find a middle ground from which to operate.

Differentiating Assessment.   With this understanding of the elements that make up assessment for career interventions, it may also be helpful to differentiate assessment from other activities that are familiar to career professionals. Consider how assessment of career interventions may be distinguished from research and evaluation.

Research.   Research studies are designed to test theories and hypotheses, resulting in affirmation or a reconceptualization of how we understand a particular problem or situation (Upcraft & Schuh, 2002). Researchers often keep an impartial distance from the object of their study and attempt to examine research questions from various angles. The purpose of research is to make generalizations beyond the study participants with the hopes of informing understanding of the phenomena in the world. While research methods may be used in the process of conducting an assessment, the reasons for pursuing assessment differ greatly from the reasons for pursuing research (Upcraft & Schuh, 2002).

Suskie (2009) suggests that assessment can be thought of as a special form of research known as action research, which primarily aims to "inform and improve one's own practice" (p. 13). In assessment, investigators are often directly connected to the intervention under study and aim to collect enough evidence to reasonably inform decisions and actions. It is not necessary, and often not feasible within time and resource constraints, to examine all angles of a question for nuanced understanding. Rather, assessment of career interventions acts as a guide for good practice (Upcraft & Schuh, 2002).

Evaluation.   To evaluate means to use evidence to make a judgment about quality, value, or effectiveness. Evaluation is one part of the assessment process related to collecting, analyzing, and interpreting data. In addition to evaluation, assessment involves activities such as describing career interventions, determining desired outcomes, prioritizing strategies for carrying out evaluations, and using findings. Evaluation, therefore, is one component of the broader process of assessment.

Why Assess?

Why is it necessary for career professionals to engage in assessment activities? It is commonly accepted that career services and programs make a difference for students. In fact, over 50 years of research has examined many different types of career interventions (e.g., individual counseling, career courses and computer-assisted career guidance programs) that are designed for a wide variety of students across the life span (e.g., college students, K–12 students and adults in career transition). Meta-analyses that look across research studies (e.g., Oliver & Spokane, 1988; Whiston, Brecheisen, & Stephens, 2003; Whiston, Sexton, & Lasoff, 1998) have found career interventions to be "moderately effective" (Whiston et al., 1998, p. 160) in assisting students to make and implement career choices, as evidenced by study effect sizes. A more recent meta-analysis study found large mean effect sizes for career interventions that included four or five sessions, with moderate mean effect sizes for career interventions with as few as two sessions (Brown & Ryan Krane, 2000). This finding suggests that evidence of the difference that career interventions make in students' lives can be found even when students engage in the experience for a brief period of time. Why then, should individual career professionals embrace assessment challenges when respected scholars reach conclusions such as "the question of whether career counseling works is no longer needed" (Oliver & Spokane, 1988, p. 447)?

Beyond such broad conclusions about positive effects, the research literature offers little guidance regarding what aspects of career interventions are particularly effective, for which students, and under what set of circumstances. A variety of limitations contribute to the challenges in examining career intervention outcomes, particularly as they pertain to specific student groups. Such limitations may include (a) a lack of detail describing the career interventions assessed, (b) insufficient detail regarding the client populations served, (c) short-term data collection that limits the ability to examine whether changes persist over time, and (d) the use of primarily quantitative methods that may show changes before and after a career intervention but do not provide insights into why or how changes occurred (e.g., Brown & Ryan Krane, 2000; Hughes & Karp, 2004; Oliver & Spokane, 1988; Whiston et al., 1998, 2003). Understanding the positive findings of past career intervention outcomes literature is helpful for informing directions in practice and motivating assessment work as it provides evidence that students generally can and do achieve desired outcomes through interactions with certain career interventions. Yet, career interventions are not one-size-fits-all—different students respond to career interventions in different ways, and environmental factors influence outcomes. It is the responsibility of career professionals to monitor and evaluate the effectiveness of their career interventions in their unique students and settings (Heibert, 1994). Further, career professionals need to seek ways to continuously improve their services as well as to articulate the value of the service they offer to their own service environments.

What to Assess?

This section provides a brief overview of each of the common assessment types in career services. Each assessment type is recognized for the unique and valuable contributions that it makes to the story of career services.

Needs.   Needs assessment aims to determine the programs, services, resources, and environmental conditions that support students' achievement of career development goals. This form of assessment informs the planning of career interventions to be offered; it answers the question of "what are career professionals going to do for and with students?" Needs assessments can be limited by career professionals' access (or lack of access) to potential student groups. Care should be taken to avoid the common pitfall of only assessing the needs of students who are already receiving services. It is critical to seek input from potential student groups who are not presently benefiting from service delivery in order to gain a complete picture of students' needs.

Participation.   Assessment of participation examines who is using career interventions, often describing users within demographic categories that are valued by the career office and institution (e.g., age, gender, race, ethnicity, and education level completed). Interpretation of participation data helps career professionals determine both who is being served by their interventions and who is not being served. One potential pitfall in relying heavily on participation data is the tendency to interpret results through a lens of "more is better," encouraging career professionals to forgo a focus on service quality in favor of a focus on increasing volume (e.g., reaching increasingly larger numbers of students and gathering larger numbers of resources).

Satisfaction.   Assessment of satisfaction explores participants' perceptions of the quality of career interventions. Interpretation of satisfaction data helps career professionals determine students' comfort and contentment with career intervention content and delivery. Satisfaction data can be helpful in the sense that they provide an immediate measure of how students engaged and enjoyed a particular career intervention. If students enjoyed a program, they may talk about the experience in a favorable way and may be likely to return for additional career intervention experiences. However, the limitation of satisfaction data is that it does not provide information on what students learn or gain from a career intervention. Assessing satisfaction alone does not examine a career intervention's contributions to students' achievement of career development goals or provide insights into how a career intervention may be improved to better facilitate student learning and growth (Bresciani, 2002; Bresciani, Zelna, & Anderson, 2004).

Outcomes. Assessment of career intervention outcomes measures results. When assessing outcomes, career professionals address questions such as "What does my program do? Why does it exist?" (Bresciani, 2001, para. 1). The goal of outcomes assessment is to determine to what degree students are achieving the desired outcomes and developmental milestones, as well as to what extent career interventions contribute to those achievements. Some types of outcomes assessments also provide insights into what modifications may be made to career interventions to enhance the likelihood of students achieving or exceeding desired outcomes. There are many types of outcomes that can be assessed; three examples that are prominent in the current higher education environment are introduced next.

Academic Performance Indicators. One strategy for examining outcomes has been to connect the programs and services offered by student services professionals on higher education campuses to the core academic missions of their institutions through academic performance indicators. Questions asked in a career services environment may include, "Do students who participate in career interventions...

- select a major earlier in their college career
- persist in their majors at a higher rate
- have a shorter time to degree completion
- have higher GPAs

...as opposed to their nonparticipant peers?" Assessing these academic performance outcomes offers intriguing stories to tell in today's environment of external stakeholder calls for accountability.

The downside to this type of evidence is that, while it may provide evidence of results, it offers little information about how to improve career interventions due to the distance between the career intervention that is delivered and the assessment measure that is taken. Suskie (2009) refers to outcomes such as retention, persistence, time to degree, and GPA as "indirect" measures, which offer proxy evidence that interventions have been successful, without "tangible, visible, self-explanatory, and compelling evidence of what students have and have not learned" (p. 20).

First Destinations. The collection and analysis of college graduate first-destination data (also referred to as postgraduation data and career outcomes) is an approach to outcomes assessment that involves an institution-wide perspective in higher education. In many cases, the impetus for collecting first-destination data has been driven by the external return-on-investment demands for information on the value of college degree completion that have been spurred by the rising cost of higher education, questions about educational quality, and concerns about job opportunities and underemployment of graduates (National Association of Colleges and Employers [NACE], 2012, 2014). Increased calls for first-destination data for accreditation and program review have also created heightened interest from faculty and administrators in this outcomes assessment work.

First-destination data are often collected on outcomes related to graduates' employment, continuing education, volunteer service, and military service, as well as whether graduates are still seeking their next destination. Surveys are the most common format for data collection, although alternate data collection strategies are employed such as following up with networking contacts (such as family members and faculty advisors) and searches of social networking sites (e.g., LinkedIn™). NACE (2014) made a distinction between these data collection strategies, reserving the term "survey rate" for data collected via traditional surveys and applying the term "knowledge rate" to the total "percent of graduates for which the institution has reasonable and verifiable information concerning the graduates' post-graduation career activities" (NACE, 2014, p. 6). Knowledge rate data may be gathered directly from college graduates via a survey data, as well as from searches of social media, reports from networking contacts, or any other source that is deemed as reliable.

Career professionals have been drawn into first-destination data collection conversations due to the unique role that they play connecting students and employers. Career professionals who have established first-destination data collection programs have expressed that their career centers experience "value and prestige from leading this effort on [their] campus" (J. Eckert, NACE First Destination Taskforce member, personal communication, January 17, 2014) because of the knowledge contributions that they make to academic departments and campus administration. However, similar to the academic performance indicators, the downside to this type of evidence is that it is an "indirect" outcome measure. The distance between the first destinations and specific career interventions makes it difficult to determine what contributes to successes or where to focus on improvements. For more direct measures of learning and student development, we now turn to a consideration of learning outcomes assessment.

Learning.   Learning outcomes assessment is a newer form of assessment for the career development field, only beginning to take a strong root in the mid-2000s, when the learning outcomes assessment movement gained momentum in student services with the introduction of *Learning Reconsidered* by the American College Personnel Association and National Association of Student Personnel Administrators (2004). Learning outcomes differ from academic performance indicators or first-destination outcomes because they offer direct (rather than indirect) evidence of the change that has occurred for the student as a result of participating in a career intervention. There is often a close tie between the career intervention and both (a) the construct or behavior being measured (e.g., improved résumé writing skills and increased career decision-making self-efficacy) and (b) the time in which the measurement is taken. These characteristics of learning outcomes assessments make them particularly useful for providing compelling evidence of the influence of career interventions as well as for using findings for continuous improvement.

Learning is "the process of transforming experiences, both past and present, into acquired knowledge, skills, and values that can be applied to future endeavors" (Makela & Rooney, 2012, p. 7). A focus on learning outcomes assessment is a special case of outcomes assessment in general. The assessment questions change from "What does my program do?" to questions about what students gain from participating in career interventions, including: (a) "how will students change as a result of what we do?," (b) "how will students be different after the intervention?," and (c) "how will students grow, change, or learn?" (Makela & Rooney, 2012, p. 8). Learning outcomes encourage career professionals to ask what students should be able to know, do, demonstrate, or feel as a result of engaging in a learning experience that is provided by a career intervention. Recognizing the central place of learning in their work, career professionals can view themselves as educators who help students learn career exploration, career decision making, and career management skills that they will use throughout their lifetime (Fried, 2006). Career interventions become educational opportunities that career professionals design and deliver for the purpose of facilitating student learning.

To assess learning, career professionals essentially aim to gather evidence of how students have changed over time. While the prospect of doing so is undoubtedly more challenging than some of the other assessment types (e.g., collecting data on program participation or participant satisfaction), there are resources and tools available to assist career professionals. One such tool is the Assessment of Learning Outcomes for Interventions (ALOI, pronounced "alloy") Cycle that is an eight-step process for conducting learning outcomes assessments that is specifically tailored to career services environments (Makela & Rooney, 2012). Table 5.1 provides a brief outline of each step. Other useful texts for guiding practitioners through learning outcomes assessment come from student affairs and higher education literature, such as Bresciani et al. (2004) and Suskie (2009).

Seeking Balance.   Each of the different assessment types presented here has value and adds unique contributions of evidence to the story about effectiveness of career interventions that career professionals want to tell (see Table 5.2). Seeking a balance across the assessment types is encouraged. Which assessment type is likely to provide the most helpful information for continuous improvement? Which assessment type is likely to provide the most persuasive evidence to share with key stakeholders? What combination of assessment types will lead to a compelling story of the effectiveness of a particular career intervention?

Needs assessment, participation tracking, and satisfaction will always have a place in our assessment work. These assessment strategies make essential contributions to the story of our career development interventions. However, the story is incomplete and the lessons learned are limited

Table 5.1. Overview of Steps in the Assessment of Learning Outcomes for Interventions Cycle

ALOI Cycle Step	Summary
1. Defining context	Describe the career intervention of interest, intended student groups, and primary stakeholders. Draw connections to relevant mission statements.
2. Brainstorming outcomes	Brainstorm possible learning outcomes, considering what students will be able to know, do, demonstrate, value, or feel following the career intervention. What difference will the career intervention make?
3. Writing outcomes statements	Transform brainstormed outcomes into learning outcomes statements that can be assessed.
4. Connecting theories and professional standards	Connect career interventions and learning outcomes statements to relevant theories and professional standards. Make additions and changes as necessary.
5. Prioritizing learning outcomes	Prioritize a limited number of learning outcomes to assess. Reserve other learning outcomes for future assessment projects.
6. Evaluating learning outcomes	Explore evaluation tools that are well-suited to assessing your learning outcomes statements. Consider possible data sources and available evaluation skills and expertise. Address ethical considerations. Carry out data collection and analysis.
7. Reflecting on results and process	Interpret results of data analysis and the assessment process, welcoming insights from a variety of stakeholders.
8. Using learning outcomes assessment	Determine uses of results, considering what will be communicated for advocacy, what will be modified or adapted, what will be discontinued, and what will be explored further in future assessments. Clearly define and implement next steps.

Source: Makela and Rooney (2012).

without the assessment of program outcomes, and learning outcomes in particular (Bresciani et al., 2004). As suggested by Keeling and associates (2007), a focus on learning outcomes fundamentally changes how career professionals think about planning and assessing career development interventions. Instead of thinking about the process of getting work done, learning outcomes assessment encourages career professionals to focus on results. Assessment efforts, rather than focusing on counting participants and determining satisfaction, become concerned with documenting changes and demonstrating results. The assessment of learning outcomes provides both (a) rich evidence of the difference that our interventions make in students' lives and (b) detailed information regarding how to increase the influence of our efforts. Learning outcomes assessment offers distinct

Table 5.2. Questions Addressed by Each Assessment Type

Assessment Type	Questions Asked
Needs	• What are career professionals going to do for and with students?
Participation	• Who did (or did not) participate in the career intervention?
Satisfaction	• How comfortable or content were participants? • How engaged were participants?
Outcomes	• What do my career intervention(s) do? • Why do they exist?
First destinations	• What are the employment, continuing education, and service outcomes of graduating students? • What might influence graduates' success in these areas?
Academic performance indicators	• How does my career intervention contribute to the academic mission and performance of the institution?
Learning	• How will students change as a result of what we do? • How will students be different after the career intervention? • How will students grow, change, or learn?

advantages for enhancing the evidence that career professionals can share about the quality of their career interventions.

Motivating Assessment

Engaging in assessment of career interventions is a desirable, and even necessary, task if career professionals are to improve their students' experiences and to advocate for the value of their work. The clearest path to achieving the goal of engaging in assessment is to make it a part of the day-to-day work of career professionals. When assessment is seen as an additional task tacked onto already overloaded schedules, it is viewed as a drain on time, resources, and energy. For assessment to be successful, staff time and resources need to be committed to this purpose. In recent years, some university career centers have integrated full-time, dedicated assessment and research positions into practice environments with the expressed goal of examining the value of career services and professional development of college students (see, e.g., the career services offices at University of Illinois at Urbana-Champaign, University of Colorado Boulder, and Colorado State University-Fort Collins). Regardless of the staffing model, a culture of assessment is needed to break down barriers and change negative perceptions regarding assessment. This section provides suggestions for motivating career professionals to engage in assessment practice.

Leaders Create Safe Spaces.   Leaders set the tone for assessment in their organizations. Setting a positive, inquiry-based tone for assessment is essential for encouraging career professionals to get involved. Traditionally, a primary barrier to assessment has been the fear of consequences (e.g., Suskie, 2009; Wehlburg, 2008). Career professionals may wonder: Will resources be taken away if the assessment results are less than stellar? Might I be blamed for weaknesses revealed by the assessment? Might punitive actions be taken? For career professionals to embrace assessment, leadership must clearly demonstrate that assessment is valued as an endeavor to improve student development (e.g., Banta, 2004; Seagraves & Dean, 2010). Results are used to recognize successes where appropriate. When changes are required for continuous improvement, career professionals determine how to use their interpretations of assessment results to modify career interventions. Leaders also recognize that some assessments may yield unanticipated results, while others may not indicate clear directions for continuous improvement. In these situations, leaders can help career professionals by guiding additional explorations of the data, supporting revised assessment efforts that may provide additional information, or encouraging a change or improvement in the career intervention. Such a flexible approach creates an environment that encourages career professionals to engage innovation, revision, and risk taking within a safe space to explore strengths and weaknesses of career interventions.

Assess Winners First.   When deciding which assessment project to begin with, select a career intervention that career professionals already anticipate to be successful. Beginning with signature or "proud programs" (Campbell, 1984, p. 37) is a strategy that helps build momentum. Career professionals can be motivated by the opportunity to test out their assumptions. Do the data demonstrate that the career intervention is as successful as expected? How can the successful career intervention be made even stronger or more meaningful? Additionally, uncovering assessment evidence that supports a favored career intervention provides a positive experience that builds career professionals' self-efficacy for pursuing future assessment endeavors. Finally, starting with successful career interventions engenders a spirit of trust that assessment is centrally about growth, learning, and celebration (Coghlan, Preskill, & Catsambas, 2003), and not primarily focused on cutting underperforming programs and services.

Use Results.   In terms of a cost–benefit analysis, the most expensive assessment (financially, physically, and emotionally) is the one that sits on the shelf and is never applied to practice (Swing & Coogan, 2010). Assessments that are completed and filed away, without reflecting on findings and creating specific strategies to use the results, are empty exercises that drain resources and diminish motivation to engage in future assessment activities. For this reason, it is essential to make time, space, and commitments to use assessments.

NEW DIRECTIONS FOR STUDENT SERVICES • DOI: 10.1002/ss

The dual purposes of assessment for continuous improvement and accountability suggest a variety of uses for findings. Focusing on the purpose of continuous improvement, the findings of assessment efforts may be used to consider how career interventions may be modified, enhanced, or discontinued in order to enhance the quality of that career intervention for a unique group of students (Seagraves & Dean, 2010; Suskie, 2009; Wehlburg, 2008). Additionally, findings may be shared with students and other stakeholders (e.g., administration, employers, faculty, and parents) to help them gain awareness of career services' value and offerings to make informed decisions about how to engage those services in the future.

Focusing on accountability, findings may be shared in a variety of forums including annual reports, staff meetings, news stories, and presentations at professional meetings. Another strategy is to offer an annual event to discuss assessment efforts, with an award program or other opportunity to share results with key stakeholders. The ultimate goal of these communications is to find tangible and meaningful ways to recognize and applaud career professionals who take on the challenge of integrating assessment into day-to-day practice. The value of their efforts can be experienced through observing enhancements to current career interventions, sharing success stories with key stakeholders, and finding opportunities to honor individuals for their contributions to enhancing the value of career services.

How to Get Started

The first key to carrying out successful assessment projects is simply to get started (Makela & Rooney, 2012; Suskie, 2009). It is too easy to become trapped in a loop of continuous planning to conduct the perfect assessment. There is no perfect assessment plan, evaluation design, interpretation of findings, and so on (Bresciani et al., 2004; Suskie, 2009). Assessment gains momentum when career professionals embrace the process and take action.

While it is beyond the scope of this chapter to demonstrate how to carry out assessments with the use of specific evaluation strategies and tools (e.g., surveys, rubrics, document analysis, interviews, and focus groups), there are a number of resources that we have found very helpful in our own practitioner-led assessment efforts, including Bresciani et al. (2004), Makela and Rooney (2012), Schuh and Upcraft (2001), and Suskie (2009). The best advice that we can offer those who are venturing into new assessment projects and plans is to begin small and undertake practical assessment projects that can, as much as possible, be integrated into day-to-day work and interactions with students (Suskie, 2009). For example, limit the number of career interventions to assess at one time or conduct assessments of career interventions on a multiyear cycle allowing time between data collection periods to fully implement suggested improvements so that changes may be measured in the repeated assessment (Swing & Coogan, 2010). Encourage assessment that is simple, yet systematic, and provides useful information. The ultimate goal is to keep expectations for assessment projects realistic (Seagraves & Dean, 2010; Suskie, 2009). Assessments are not meant to be research efforts that are generalized to other populations. Rather, assessments collect enough evidence to reasonably inform the decisions and actions taken in a specific practice environment with a unique group of students (Suskie, 2009).

In the long run, career services offices are best served by conducting a few, focused, high-quality assessments (as opposed to many, rushed, poorly implemented assessments). Think of assessing career interventions in terms of building a house. Focus on laying one brick at a time, no matter how small, and building up a strong foundation—a rich body of evidence (Makela & Rooney, 2012). Telling an assessment story in a series of small chapters can be a powerful and meaningful strategy.

References

American College Personnel Association and National Association of Student Personnel Administrators. (2004). *Learning reconsidered: A campus-wide focus on the student experience*. Washington, DC: Author.

Banta, T. W. (Ed.). (2004). *Hallmarks of effective outcomes assessment*. San Francisco, CA: Wiley.

Bresciani, M. J. (2001, October 16). Writing measureable and meaningful outcomes. *NetResults*. Retrieved from http://www.naspa.org

Bresciani, M. J. (2002, December 9). Outcomes assessment in student affairs: Moving beyond satisfaction to student learning and development. *NetResults*. Retrieved from http://www.naspa.org

Bresciani, M. J., Zelna, C. L., & Anderson, J. A. (2004). *Assessing student learning and development: A handbook for practitioners*. Washington, DC: National Association of Student Personnel Administrators.

Brown, S. D., & Ryan Krane, N. E. (2000). Four (or five) sessions and a cloud of dust: Old assumptions and new observations about career counseling. In S. D. Brown & R. W. Lent (Eds.), *Handbook of counseling psychology* (3rd ed., pp. 740–766). New York, NY: Wiley.

Campbell, D. T. (1984). Can we be scientific in applied social science? In R. F. Conner, D. G. Altman, & C. Jackson (Eds.), *Evaluation studies: Review annual* (Vol. 9, pp. 26–48). Beverly Hills, CA: Sage.

Coghlan, A. T., Preskill, H., & Catsambas, T. T. (2003). An overview of appreciative inquiry in evaluation. In H. Preskill & A. T. Coghlan (Eds.), *New Directions for Evaluation: No. 100. Using appreciative inquiry in evaluation* (pp. 5–22). New York, NY: Wiley.

Ewell, P. T. (2009). *Assessment, accountability, and improvement: Revisiting the tension*. Champaign, IL: National Institute for Learning Outcomes Assessment, University of Illinois and Indiana University.

Fried, J. (2006). Rethinking learning. In R. P. Keeling (Ed.), *Learning reconsidered 2: A practical guide to implementing a campus-wide focus on the student experience* (pp. 3–9). Washington, DC: American College Personnel Association.

Guskin, A. E. (1994). Reducing student costs and enhancing student learning. *Change*, 26(4), 22–30.

Heibert, B. (1994). A framework for quality control, accountability, and evaluation: Being clear about the legitimate concerns of career counseling. *Canadian Journal of Counseling, 28*(4), 334–345.

Hughes, K. L., & Karp, M. M. (2004). *School-based career development: A synthesis of literature.* New York, NY: Institute on Education and the Economy, Teachers College, Columbia University.

Keeling, R. P., & Associates. (2007, June). *Putting Learning Reconsidered into practice: Developing and assessing student learning outcomes.* Workshop presented at the National Association of Student Personnel Administrators' Learning Reconsidered Institute, St. Louis, MO.

Makela, J. P., & Rooney, G. S. (2012). *Learning outcomes assessment step-by-step: Enhancing evidence-based practice in career services.* Broken Arrow, OK: National Career Development Association.

National Association of Colleges and Employers (NACE). (2012, July). *Position statement: The critical importance of institutional first-destination/post-graduation surveys.* Retrieved from http://www.naceweb.org/advocacy/position-statements/first-destination-surveys.aspx

National Association of Colleges and Employers (NACE). (2014, January). *Standards and protocols for the collection and dissemination of graduating student initial career outcomes information for undergraduates.* Retrieved from http://www.naceweb.org/uploadedFiles/Pages/advocacy/first-destination-survey-standards-and-protocols.pdf

Oliver, L. W., & Spokane, A. R. (1988). Career-intervention outcome: What contributes to client gain? *Journal of Counseling Psychology, 35*(4), 447–462.

Schuh, J. H., & Gansemer-Topf, A. M. (2010). *The role of student affairs in student learning assessment.* Champaign, IL: National Institute for Learning Outcomes Assessment, University of Illinois and Indiana University.

Schuh, J. H., & Upcraft, M. L. (2001). *Assessment practice in student affairs: An applications manual.* San Francisco, CA: Jossey-Bass.

Seagraves, B., & Dean, L. S. (2010). Conditions supporting a culture of assessment in student affairs divisions at small colleges and universities. *Journal of Student Affairs Research and Practice, 47*(3), 307–324.

Shulman, L. S. (2007). Counting and recounting: Assessment and the quest for accountability. *Change, 39*(1), 20–25.

Suskie, L. (2009). *Assessing student learning: A common sense guide* (2nd ed.). San Francisco, CA: Jossey-Bass.

Swing, R. L., & Coogan, C. S. (2010). *Valuing assessment: Cost–benefit considerations.* Champaign, IL: National Institute for Learning Outcomes Assessment, University of Illinois and Indiana University.

Upcraft, M. L., & Schuh, J. H. (1996). *Assessment in student affairs: A guide for practitioners.* San Francisco, CA: Jossey-Bass.

Upcraft, M. L., & Schuh, J. H. (2002). Assessment vs. research: Why we should care about the difference. *About Campus, 7*(1), 16–20.

U.S. Department of Education. (2006). *A test of leadership: Charting the future of American higher education* (Report of the commission appointed by the Secretary of Education Margaret Spellings). Washington, DC: Author.

Wehlburg, C. M. (2008). *Promoting integrated and transformative assessment: A deeper focus on student learning.* San Francisco, CA: Jossey-Bass.

Whiston, S. C., Brecheisen, B. K., & Stephens, J. (2003). Does treatment modality affect career counseling effectiveness? *Journal of Vocational Behavior, 62*, 390–410.

Whiston, S. C., Sexton, T. L., & Lasoff, D. L. (1998). Career-intervention outcome: A replication and extension of Oliver and Spokane. *Journal of Counseling Psychology, 45*, 150–165.

The White House. (2013, August 22). *Fact sheet on the President's plan to make college more affordable: A better bargain for the middle class* (Press Release). Retrieved from

http://www.whitehouse.gov/the-press-office/2013/08/22/fact-sheet-president-s-plan
-make-college-more-affordable-better-bargain-
Wingspread Group on Higher Education. (1993). *An American imperative: Higher expectations for higher education*. Racine, WI: Johnson Foundation.

JULIA PANKE MAKELA *is an associate director of Assessment and Research at the
Career Center, University of Illinois at Urbana-Champaign.*

GAIL S. ROONEY *is an associate dean of Leadership and Career Development,
University of Illinois at Urbana-Champaign.*

NEW DIRECTIONS FOR STUDENT SERVICES • DOI: 10.1002/ss

6

The chapter will focus on the role of career services in external relations. It will provide the basis for this connection along with best practices in developing and maintaining a mutually beneficial relationship between career centers and on-campus and off-campus partners.

Career Services in University External Relations

Seth C. W. Hayden, Katherine E. Ledwith

Over time, career services offices in higher education have grown from job placement centers to a place offering a more comprehensive model of services (Herr, Rayman, & Garis, 1993; Hoover, Lenz, & Garis, 2013; Niles & Harris-Bowlsbey, 2012). Because career centers in colleges and universities range widely in size, organizational structure, mission, funding, staff, and number of students served, the type of services offered at each office also varies. The 2013–2014 National Association of Colleges and Universities (NACE) Career Services Benchmark Survey for Colleges and Universities found that more than 50% of the respondents provided career counseling by appointment, as well as career fairs, workshops, on-campus interview programs, assistance to students pursuing employer-offered internship, co-op, or externship opportunities, and career resources and assessments. Other less offered services included academic advising, career courses for credit, and credential files (NACE, 2014a). These services operate in partnership with many vital stakeholders. Arguably, career services is the higher education unit with the most contact with external constituents due to its unique and central role between students, alumni, parents, employers, and all other entities of a community. The NACE (2014b) "Professional Standards for College and University Career Services" noted that as an integral function within the institution, "career services must develop and maintain productive relationships with relevant campus offices and key stakeholders at the institution and externally" (Section VIII). However, career services professionals may wonder why they should dedicate resources to building external relations in light of competing priorities and limited resources.

On an institutional level, national, ongoing reductions in state funding have created a growing focus on colleges and universities for recruitment and retention (Fain, 2009; Mactaggart, 2007). Studies link student

NEW DIRECTIONS FOR STUDENT SERVICES, no. 148, Winter 2014 © 2014 Wiley Periodicals, Inc.
Published online in Wiley Online Library (wileyonlinelibrary.com) • DOI: 10.1002/ss.20110

career development and defined career goals with increased satisfaction and retention rates (Feldman, 2005; Hull-Banks et al., 2005). Through off-campus partnerships, career centers have the potential to connect students and alumni with a wide range of career experiences such as part-time jobs, internships, and career fairs, in turn supporting local and nonlocal economic development efforts. This chapter will explore the various groups of interest to career centers and offer suggestions for building and developing effective partnerships.

External Relations

Career centers often engage in significant activity designed to enhance engagement with external entities such as employers, faculty, and students. External relations, as discussed here, include both on-campus and off-campus entities; in other words, any partnership formed with an individual or organizations outside of the career center. Recognized professional standards associated with guiding the activity of university career centers with regard to external relations focus largely on interactions with employers, faculty, and alumni (NACE, 2014b). However, they also note that "career services must work collaboratively with academic divisions, departments, individual faculty members, student services, employers, and other relevant constituencies of the institution to enhance students' career development" (NACE, 2014b, Section II). While effective management of these relationships is critical to providing quality services, connecting to the broader community presents the potential for beneficial reciprocal partnerships.

On-Campus Partners

Career services must strategically develop relationships with both on-campus partners and others external to the university such as employers, community members, and other colleges and universities.

Faculty. Students are provided support from a number of on-campus personnel, including faculty. Depending on the institution, faculty may be more or less involved in advising a student's individual career development process; some faculty members carry a teaching load and function as the departmental internship coordinator. However, career center staff can encourage faculty to connect with career services in a variety of ways. For example, the University of California San Diego Career Services has created a specific page on their website for faculty titled "How to Collaborate With the Career Services Center," providing guidance to faculty on how best to integrate the career center into their work (http://career.ucsd.edu/faculty/collaborating-career.html). At University of California San Diego, faculty can be offered (and request) classroom presentations from career services on career development topics related to the academic topics (e.g., "Internships for International Affairs").

Career center personnel can create a "career-friendly" faculty directory for assisting students in locating faculty members willing to assist with career development needs, such as identifying industry and alumni contacts, recommending career resources, and/or major-specific experiential opportunities.

Class assignments or extra credit options such as résumé critiques, mock interviews, or career center scavenger hunts could be incorporated into the syllabus. Faculty can play an important role in writing letters of recommendation for students for professional and graduate school opportunities.

As faculty speak with students and advise student organizations on career development topics, career center staff may need to increase faculty awareness of ethical guidelines such as the National Association of Colleges and Employers (NACE) "Professional Standards for College and University Career Services" to guide how best to refer students and employers to job opportunities. To build relationships with faculty, career center staff can offer college or department open houses at the career center, attend and share career center events at faculty meetings, and invite faculty to attend and/or participate in career center events such as fairs, panels, and advisory boards. Data from student surveys on the career development needs or postgraduation or employment outcomes for specific colleges or majors could be another area of discussion and collaboration for future efforts.

Academic Advising.   Academic advising is a universal process for college and university students, whether accomplished through faculty, staff, or designated advising professionals. Collaboration with academic advising offices concerning the career and academic concerns of students is a logical outcome of an advising process that looks at both immediate academic needs and future occupational goals. While a quarter of career services offices already offer academic advising (mostly at associate's level institutions), many career services and advising professionals will be required to be intentional about reaching out to their university colleagues (NACE, 2014a).

Recent examples for academic and career services collaboration can be found in "Purposeful Partnerships for Student Career Success: Student Affairs and Academic Affairs Collaboration," which examines 10 distinctive partnerships across the California State University System, highlighting collaboration between career centers and academic programs that support student success (The California State University, 2011). In one instance, the Career Center at CalPoly Pomona created a designated liaison role between the career center and the Collins School of Hospitality Management. In this position, the career services liaison developed career education programs, networked with employers to create employment opportunities, and utilized career assessments for hospitality students, the success of which inspired the intent to pursue joint-liaison-funded positions for other colleges. Other partnerships between career services and academic affairs at other schools included collaborative employer surveys, practice interviews, internship fairs, academic-career education modules, and intentional advising/career checkpoints.

Academic and career offices are uniquely situated to collaborate on specific populations (e.g., first-year or exploratory students) as a shared approach to more time-intensive student groups is potentially cost and resource effective. Career interventions such as career classes provide possibilities for practical integration of career development into academic curriculum, such as for-credit general career development courses or career courses designed for a specific population, such as undergraduate-level communication majors. Shared communication and referrals on both sides can assist in spreading the word about possible assistance; career center staff can provide academic advisors with packets of flyers and schedules of career center events, marketing materials, and career center information to share with students. Chapter 4 offers further suggestions for best collaborative practices with academic advising.

Civic Engagement.   There is an increasing trend across the country regarding the integration of community engagement in the college students' academic experience. Civic engagement is defined as "university actors working in the community they serve," and for students specifically, engaging through "service-learning and other co-curricular activities" (Moore & Mendez, 2014, p. 33). Similarly, there is an increasing need for strategic partnerships between career centers and civic engagement offices (if such an office is not already incorporated within the mission of the career center). By creating "one-stop shops" for students and especially employers, where student volunteer opportunities are listed in the same office as other experiential opportunities, whether service learning, internships, part-time jobs, etc., career services offices can conveniently provide a single and comprehensive location for experiential learning opportunities.

Some college and university career centers have already enacted such a formal functional approach between civic engagement and career services offices. For example, the "Center for Community Engagement and Career Education" at the University of California-Bakersfield (https://www.csub.edu/cece/) houses both volunteer and career opportunities. Such approaches, whether formal or informal, support professional standards, stating that career services should help students "link with alumni, employers, professional organizations, and others who will provide opportunities to develop professional interests and competencies, integrate academic learning with work, and explore future career possibilities" (NACE, 2014b, Section I).

Career center staff collaborate with civic education colleagues to make appropriate referrals (if housed in separate offices), promote civic engagement opportunities when talking with students as an option to learn more about self or knowledge, and assist students in articulating skills and knowledge gained as a result of civic engagement and service learning on résumés, cover letters, and interviews. Civic experience can also be suggested as a valuable addition to résumés for professional and graduate school applications.

Alumni.   Hoover et al. (2013) noted that "forging effective relationships with alumni is a goal of all higher education institutions" (p. 76) and that an alumni's career center is often the first place a former student will turn to in case of unemployment or career difficulties after graduation. Because of this, and the financial impact of alumni for colleges and universities on rankings, alumni are an important constituent of career services in higher education (Barron, 2013).

Several models exist for career centers working to assist alumni with their career development needs. Career centers can offer full or limited services (e.g., access to certain services such as online job databases, on-campus recruiting, and mock interviewing is denied after a specified time limit). Others have specific career services offices and dedicated staff to work with alumni (e.g., see the University of Virginia's Alumni Association Career Services office). An alumni liaison role within the main career center office could be created to develop relationships with key staff in the alumni office, serve as a conduit for information about events and resources, and assist in shaping the direction of career services for this population. For the most effective work, Hoover et al. (2013) advised career services to reach out to specific alumni groups (e.g., a geographically based alumni group or alumni from a specific major or college), as well as connecting via social media, a commonly utilized networking tool for alumni. In the NACE (2014a) Benchmark Survey, services offered to alumni included job listings (97.2%), career counseling (93.7%), résumé referral services (65.7%), testing services (54.6%), and workshops (64.5%). Fees for access to these services are another consideration for the career center.

Such programming with and for alumni can be mutually beneficial. For example, a partnering at Binghamton University between the Center for Career and Professional Development and the Alumni Association for Networking Nights in New York City provides benefits to students and alumni alike (Seepersaud, 2014). At the event, students learn career development tips and advice, and alumni can promote and leverage their businesses. Alumni have much to offer to career centers and current students, and professional standards dictate that career centers "arrange appropriate programs that use alumni experience and expertise" (NACE, 2014b, Section VIII). Alumni can offer recent perspectives on job searching in the current job market and can provide valuable insights for professional networking programs, panels, and workshops. Ongoing inquiries of an institution's alumni regarding their vocational situation provide valuable information for career center staff serving alumni as well as enhancing career services for current students.

Educational Institutions

In addition to involvement with alumni, one of the factors that contributes to the success of a college or university career center is partnerships with other career-related local, state, and national organizations. Sampson, Reardon, Peterson, and Lenz (2004) stated that understanding boundary spanning in the context of strategic planning is an effective way for a career center to support its programs as connected to other area organizations and to "maintain and enhance the viability of a program in a broader organizational and environmental context" (p. 290). Strategic planning, as related to community partnerships, is an important way to identify external resources to enhance the career center as well as the student population it serves.

Because of a shared organizational focus on student learning, one of the most obvious partners for a college or university career center is career services personnel at local educational institutions. A common theory underlying career program goals and outcomes for many career development practitioners is that of Donald Super who believed that career development, including job searching, was a lifelong process (Super, 1980). Practically speaking, then, career development education can often begin formally for a student in elementary school and continue through to college or university (Niles & Harris-Bowlsbey, 2012). Higher education career center staff can provide assistance to school counselors in elementary, middle, and high schools to support career competencies who may not have access to specialized career resources or tools. In addition, career centers open to the community can conduct workshops for these students, raising career awareness before reaching college. For example, at Florida State University, career center staff have presented at high school assemblies and have tabled at their career fairs to provide more information about majors and occupations, and local and state-wide career resources available to them (such as Florida Choices, www.flchoices.org). Older versions of recently updated resources from a career library could be donated to a local high school. Additionally, local sites provide internship opportunities for career counselors-in-training for primary and secondary school-aged populations.

After high school, students may potentially choose local two-year colleges, four-year colleges or universities, or technical schools, among other options. In the fall of 2012, 45% of all university freshmen matriculated from a community college (American Association of Community Colleges, 2013). Given the high volume of students attending community colleges who may strongly consider continuing their education at a four-year institution, it is important that university career centers form strong partnerships

The California State University. (2011, January). *Purposeful partnerships for student career success: Student affairs and academic affairs collaboration.* Retrieved from http://www.fullerton.edu/Crew/projects/docs/PurposefulPartnerships.pdf

Collegiate Employment Research Institute (CERI). (2013). *Recruiting Trends 2012–2013* (43rd ed). East Lansing: Michigan State University.

Fain, P. (2009, March 31). Trustee survey paints grim budget picture over next year for public universities. *The Chronicle of Higher Education, 55*(34), A13. Retrieved from http://chronicle.com/weekly/v55/i34/34a01301.htm

Feldman, R. S. (2005). *Improving the first year of college, research and practice.* Mahwah, NJ: Lawrence Erlbaum Associates.

Hart, A., & Wolff, D. (2006). Developing local "communities of practice" through community–university partnerships. *Planning, Practice & Research, 21*(1), 121–138.

Herr, E., Rayman, J., & Garis, J. (1993). *Handbook for the college and university career center.* Westport, CT: Greenwood Press.

Hoover, M., Lenz, J., & Garis, J. (2013). *Employer relations and recruitment: An essential part of postsecondary career services.* Broken Arrow, OK: National Career Development Association.

Hull-Banks, E., Kurpius, S. E. R., Befort, C., Sollenberger, S., Nicpon, M. F., & Huser, L. (2005). Career goals and retention-related factors among college freshmen. *Journal of Career Development, 32,* 16–30. doi:10.1177/0894845305277037

Kellogg Commission on the Future of State and Land-Grant Universities. (1999). *Returning to our roots: The engaged institution* [Online]. Washington, DC: National Association of State Universities and Land-Grant Colleges. Retrieved from http://www.aplu.org/NetCommunity/Document.Doc?id=187

Mactaggart, T. (2007, October 12). The realities of rescuing colleges in distress. *The Chronicle of Higher Education, 54*(7), B11. Retrieved from http://chronicle.com/article/The-Realities-of-Rescuing/16705/

Moore, T. L., & Mendez, J. P. (2014). Civic engagement and organizational learning strategies for student success. In P. L. Eddy (Ed.), *New Directions for Higher Education: No. 165. Connecting learning across the institution* (pp. 31–40). San Francisco, CA: Jossey-Bass. doi:10.1002/he.20081

National Association of Colleges and Employers (NACE). (2013). *Professional standards for university relations and recruitment.* Retrieved from http://www.naceweb.org/knowledge/professional-standards-university-relations-recruiting.pdf

National Association of Colleges and Employers (NACE). (2014a). *NACE 2013–2014 career services benchmark survey for colleges and universities.* Bethlehem, PA: Author.

National Association of Colleges and Employers (NACE). (2014b). *Professional standards for college and university career services.* Retrieved from www.naceweb.org/knowledge/CS/professional_standards/

Niles, S. G., & Harris-Bowlsbey, J. A. (2012). *Career development interventions in the 21st century.* Upper Saddle River, NJ: Merrill/Pearson.

Sampson, J. P. (2008). *Designing and implementing career programs: A handbook for effective practice.* Broken Arrow, OK: National Career Development Association.

Sampson, J. P., Reardon, R., Peterson, G., & Lenz, J. (2004). *Career counseling and services: A cognitive information processing approach.* Belmont, CA: Thomson/Brooks/Cole.

Seepersaud, S. (2014). *Employer visit program helps students build networks, learn corporate culture.* Retrieved from http://www.binghamton.edu/alumni/news/alumni-connect/jan-2014/employer-visits.html

Super, D. (1980). A life-span, life-space approach to career development. *Journal of Vocational Behavior, 16*(3), 282–296.

Weerts, D. J., & Sandmann, L. R. (2008). Building a two-way street: Challenges and opportunities for community engagement at research universities. *Review of Higher Education*, 32(1), 73–106.

SETH C. W. HAYDEN *is an assistant professor of counseling at Wake Forest University.*

KATHERINE E. LEDWITH *is a coordinator of Pathway Advising at Pikes Peak Community College.*

NEW DIRECTIONS FOR STUDENT SERVICES • DOI: 10.1002/ss

7

This chapter emphasizes the important role career services plays in advising students about global careers.

The Globalization of Career Services

Mark A. Kenyon, Heather T. Rowan-Kenyon

As our world becomes increasingly characterized by interconnectedness and international economic as well as educational competition, there is an emerging need for global citizens who can face the challenges of a highly competitive workforce. It is increasingly important for American colleges and universities to graduate students with the knowledge, skills, and attitudes to become citizens of the world prepared to participate in the global workforce (NAFSA: Association of International Educators, 2003; Stier, 2003). Today's graduates need to be intellectually resilient, interculturally competent, and prepared for a future of lifelong learning. Understanding and effectively navigating other societies and cultures is no longer a matter of choice but has become essential for working and living successfully in a globalizing world (Morais & Ogdan, 2011).

American college students have an unprecedented range of international opportunities available to broaden their worldview and deepen their understanding of global issues. However, students too frequently accumulate international experiences in an ad hoc fashion, absent from any clear relationship to their curricular choices and unrelated to their career goals. Career services professionals need to consider ways to transform their programs and services to assist students who have an interest in becoming more global citizens.

The Globalization of Career Services

Amid this push for further internationalization, career services has entered into a new era, one in which services and staff are responding to calls to prepare their students to engage competently in a globalizing and increasingly interdependent world (Altbach & McGill Peterson, 1998; Bennett & Salonen, 2007; Cornwell & Stoddard, 2006; Nolan, 2009). There are two primary ways of increasing globalization of career services; the first is helping to match students with global career possibilities after graduation. The second is the increased need to connect students with international internships.

NEW DIRECTIONS FOR STUDENT SERVICES, no. 148, Winter 2014 © 2014 Wiley Periodicals, Inc.
Published online in Wiley Online Library (wileyonlinelibrary.com) • DOI: 10.1002/ss.20111

Global careers are built step-by-step over time. If a student wants to graduate with a global portfolio, he or she needs to acquire multiple layers of international experience throughout college. Global recruitment is an emerging trend in the international arena. Global companies and organizations find qualified candidates in different countries with diverse backgrounds. These employers require previous international experience as proof that a student can work in a cross-cultural work environment and that the student has the skills to succeed abroad. Career services professionals need to find avenues to share the expectations of international employers with students early in their college careers so that they can plan accordingly and graduate with necessary experiences.

Many career services offices have dedicated staff, but some may not have extensive international experience to draw upon when advising students about global careers. Global recruitment is different than domestic recruitment in the United States. One distinction is the need to manage the complexities of operating in a different country and culture. A major reason for failure of a global job search is a lack of understanding of the differences between one's domestic environment and a foreign one. Students have to navigate additional external factors compared to domestic job searches. Examples of these factors include government regulations about staffing practices in foreign locations, local codes of conduct, unfamiliar visa requirements and tax practices, the possible influence of local religious groups, unique résumés and curriculum vitae, diverse networks, and atypical pay rates (IHRM: International Human Resource Management, 2011).

Professionals also have a role in advising students on what international employers focus on in their global recruitment process. Students and professionals need to be knowledgeable about international business trends and be well versed in the technology used in global environments. It is important for students and professionals to understand the different job markets around the world. Certain countries have highly skilled workers and job search traditions, but each market has specializations in various fields (IHRM: International Human Resource Management, 2011).

The Internet plays a huge role in global recruiting because applicants can connect with international organizations from wherever they are. Global recruiters often use cloud computing, or software that is accessed through the Internet, to perform many of their business processes. Students need to be very comfortable working on the web to find global careers, submit applications, and stay in touch with recruiters and organizations. When working in an international environment, students will need to communicate with others who speak different languages. While students might not speak multiple languages, they should have contact with translation services during the job search to put employer marketing materials and other written communication into the native language of the applicant or employer (IHRM: International Human Resource Management, 2011).

Professionals can help students navigate the pitfalls of doing a country-specific job search and help find international recruiters in the student's areas of expertise. Professionals can also help students to research internationally focused jobs by targeting international employers in the United States who are also working in a field of interest. Many U.S.-based organizations (private firms, nongovernment organizations [NGOs], and government departments) have opportunities for students to work or travel abroad and should not be eliminated as an employment opportunity. Professionals will need to build networks of the types of employers who regularly hire recent college grads for international work (Richard, 2013).

The second opportunity area to globalize career services is to expand the availability of international internships. Prior research on international student immersion programs found that these experiences, even ones as short as 10 days, can influence students' future career choices (Jones, Rowan-Kenyon, Ireland, Niehaus, & Skendall, 2012; Rowan-Kenyon & Niehaus, 2011), and including an internship in such experiences can help to clarify career path/goals, improve understanding of social justice and globalization issues, and provide opportunities for learning and personal growth (Benedict-Augustin, 2010; Evanson & Zust, 2004). Students can build their global portfolio and work toward matching with a global career placement by acquiring an international internship. International internships add a global perspective to work and are typically five-, seven-, or ten-week experiences. The purpose of international internships is to give students an opportunity to gain work knowledge, to be exposed to an international organization's operations, and to experience acculturation through sufficient time in country (Furnham & Bockner, 1986).

International internships offer students a unique global experiential learning perspective, while maintaining the same benefits students would expect to find in a domestic internship back in the United States. These benefits include the chance to try out a career, the opportunity to bridge the gap between theory and practice, the experience of learning by doing, exposure to a professional culture and work habits, and the chance to make valuable personal and professional networking contacts. Research suggests that professionals view an international internship experience as being at least as important as foreign language training, in terms of the skills and knowledge that a person should possess to be successful as an international professional (Lundstrom, White, & Schuster, 1996; Nolting, 2008).

The types of international internships as well as international organizations that support such experiences differ widely. According to a review of international internships, Nolting (2008) found that there are three primary categories of international internships: (a) study abroad internships, (b) internship exchange/work permit programs, and (c) internships with international organizations.

Study abroad internships include hundreds of overseas internships that are sponsored by universities and colleges for undergraduate students seeking to incorporate an international internship with a study abroad experience. Advantages for students include institutional support and student services, academic credit, applicability of financial aid, and a variety of placements and locations. Disadvantages include the potential high cost and sometimes unpredictability of placement (Nolting, 2008). These internships may be a collaboration between study abroad offices and career services to develop and oversee some of these programs.

Internship exchange and work permit programs include reciprocal exchange programs offering internships in applied fields. There are a number of international organizations that facilitate the process for U.S. and other international students to obtain work permits, such as the Association Internationale des Étudiants en Sciences Économiques et Commerciales (AIESEC) and the British University North American Club (BUNAC). These programs aim to develop leadership capacities, encourage a better understanding among students from different nations, and promote the advancement of learning and education of students. However, students need to be diligent in the process. For most of these international organizations the visas you receive require the recipient to be a student. The visas are generally 4–12 months and once they run out you must leave the country (BUNAC, 2012; Nolting, 2008; Reinholt, 2012).

Internships with international organizations are the third type of international internship, often with a centralized formal application process. Larger and better known organizations, such as the United Nations and the World Bank, tend to have a competitive application process for unpaid internships. Private global enterprises such as Proctor & Gamble, Coca-Cola, and IBM all have well-designed international internship programs (IIE, 2009; Nolting, 2008).

Smaller and more locally based and community-based organizations, such as G.R.A.C.E. in Kenya, BAID Foundation in China, and Comunitas in Brazil, may offer some of the best internship experiences. Another example of a more locally based program is the U.S. Government. The U.S. Department of State and other federal agencies have offices overseas and in the United States offering internships for undergraduate and graduate students to work locally with community-based organizations (Green, 2012; Nolting, 2008). NGOs are often another provider of international internships. These organizations often have unpaid internships available including Amnesty International, CARE, the Bermuda Biological Station, and the Institute of International Education.

Finally, private voluntary organizations (PVOs) offer many overseas internship placements and are one of the only possibilities for interning in developing countries. Positions are typically designated as "volunteer" or service positions, rather than internships. These service positions can be found in secular organizations, such as Amigos de las Americas or WorldTeach, and in religious-sponsored groups. Short-term placements (of less than one year) will often charge fees, or at best provide room and board. Despite organizations' provision of positions, most undergraduates arrange international internships on their own. These self-developed opportunities take initiative but also allow for flexibility in the experience. Students conduct the required research on their own, contact local organizations in the host country of their choice, and set up opportunities (IIE, 2009; Nolting, 2008). Student placements at PVOs can be a challenge for career services professionals because there are varying degrees of safety in these developing countries and there can be a lack of oversight over the position. It is also a challenge for the bandwidth of career professionals to help develop these types of positions.

Recommendations for Practitioners

How can career services departments and career counselors on our university campuses create an environment that nurtures promising individuals and allows future knowledge workers to compete globally? The following recommendations, based on the experience of the authors, represent areas career services departments can use in thinking about globalization and the internationalization of their services, institutions, and communities.

1. The internationalization of campus and community is both an opportunity and a challenge that must be embraced.

   Career services professionals should consider the following when planning to strategically globalize. Key questions to consider:

   - What kind of careers are emerging in today's interconnected world relevant to our students, where are they emerging, and how do we prepare our students and communities for them?
   - How can our career services departments and universities as a whole achieve an enhanced international presence?
   - How can institutions of higher education and career services be positioned for success in today's global environment and what role should local, regional, national, and international partners play?

2. Vision matters—career services staff and infrastructure are only part of the success equation.

   Globally focused career centers need to let the world know they have a purpose and a vision concerning what they are and what they seek to become. Globally focused career services departments have two central responsibilities in society today: (a) enlightening and preparing, not just their students, but their respective communities as a whole for the challenges and opportunities brought on by globalization; and (b) being the major supplier of the intellectual capital (knowledge workers) that communities need to survive and prosper in the era of globalization. Without solid top-level visionary underpinnings, most exercises in internationalization are treated like "step children," allowed at the table but never given equal status with others, and thus, never really influential in terms of campus culture or community impact (Green, 2014).

3. Effective globally focused career services establish broad policies and priorities related to innovative initiatives aimed at developing a global culture throughout their campus and community.

For almost all universities that embraced significant international programs, there were clearly delineated "guiding principles" that defined where priorities would lie, how efforts related to such priorities would be supported, and how success would be rewarded. Clearly stated policies and resulting priorities can lead to a myriad of noteworthy international initiatives. These initiatives include exceptional visiting scholar support, unique degree and nondegree certification options, distinctive overseas study agendas, exclusive international internships, innovative student scholarships, part-time job options in the international arena, outstanding cross-disciplinary grant opportunities for faculty, and promising overseas partnerships (Green, 2014).

Getting meaningful global initiatives off the ground will typically be accompanied by broad-based "buy-ins," beginning with the top university leadership, but also including deans and department heads at specific schools, directors of centers, individual faculty members, students, and the broader community-based leadership as well. It is important for career services staff to be part of these initiatives and promote collaborations with others and develop partnerships.

4. Exemplary globally focused programs and initiatives succeed or fail based primarily on the dedication and capability of their champions: their creative entrepreneurs.

Among the universities and colleges, the role of faculty and campus leaders is seen as central and critical to an institution's embrace of globalization. While many internationally focused programs tend to have a clear vision of what they hope to accomplish, along with solid backing from the president and other key leaders (as well as a dedicated and skilled support staff), it was a motivated, entrepreneurial faculty and staff, more so than any other component, which drove international success. Universities must create a team of dedicated, internationally focused faculty and career services professionals, give them responsibility for initiatives, and then get out of their way and reward them for superior effort and results. Globally focused career services teams can come from many different places, including one's own campus, overseas institutions, alliances of multiple institutions, or the cross-functional teams of faculty, international education, study abroad, and career services staff members.

5. Students are central to the success of any university's attempt to globalize its campus and community, and students are the primary reason
why a university should embrace internationalization.

   A widely held tenet is that if students are to fully assume positions of leadership and responsibility in specific organizations and in
society as a whole, then they must be prepared to work in a global environment. Both domestic and international students must be woven
into any institution's "international fabric" if a genuinely globalized
on-campus and community-wide environment is to be achieved.

   It has been the experience of the first author that institutions with
outstanding international programs are those that cultivate an underlying philosophy of providing an international environment and
international experience for all their students. This requires a con-
certed focus on both international students studying on campus and
domestic students studying abroad. It also requires dedicated efforts
by faculty and administrators to create innovative on-campus courses,
programs, and events of learning that allow both international and domestic students to interact with one another and to think outside their
regional or national "boxes." It also requires strategic alliances with
the outside communities that envelop a university and bring a "real-
world" dimension to the initiatives and programs undertaken on be-
half of students. The more successful institutions tend to view themselves as an education service provider with the larger community
being their customer, and the student being their "raw material" that
is being shaped, molded, and guided in order to eventually achieve excellence in the global arena. Most understand that making their students receptive to this view depends on what they offer in the way
of globally relevant education and experience opportunities and how
they cater to and provide services related to their global education and
career services (Green, 2014; Nolan, 2009).

6. No career services department is an island. Partnerships and alliances
are critical components of international educational development and
a global focus.

   The value of university partnerships (whether they are developed by the university as a whole, or contained within various colleges, schools, career services departments, or programs) with local,
regional, national, and international communities is well understood
by leaders in higher education. Partnerships or alliances can take
on many forms including those with other institutions of education
(within the United States and overseas), within a framework of a con-
sortium of universities (again, within the United States and overseas),
with a university and its alumni (both U.S.-based and international),
and with a university and various for-profit, not-for-profit, govern-
mental, nongovernmental, and other types of organizations. The list

of possibilities is truly limited only by a university's vision and corresponding goals. These partnerships can also help staff to gain knowledge and experiences to use in their work with students.

The goals of university–community alliances can vary widely, including enhancing the content and array of educational offerings, recruiting new students and faculty, and raising funds or developing streams of revenues to support mutual aspirations such as building a shared global reputation as a progressive and engaged community. The focus of the university career services department should not be location, location, location, but relation, relation, relation. A central ingredient to strong international programs is the establishment of meaningful relationships based on common values and goals and a sense of trust between partners. In today's globalized world, this reality has never been more important.

7. The organization behind a university's career services department's international efforts appears to work best when it is both centralized and decentralized.

The most prominent commonality among career services departments that exhibit progressive and innovative approaches to their international programs, initiatives, and alliances is the organizational structure that guides their efforts. Both centralized and decentralized dimensions are apparent. On the one hand, the majority of institutions had a centralized "one-stop" office for administering, advising, coordinating, implementing, and maintaining all international activities.

On the other hand, it was apparent that while information on almost all international programs could be found in the centralized international office, most successful international programs are championed by a specific faculty (or individual) of a specific school, department, center, or other decentralized branch of an institution along with career services. In general, innovative initiatives tended to have clearly designated individuals with known "creative" expertise who developed, promoted, managed, maintained, and continually sought to improve a given program. Such "champions" tended to passionately advance their programs by actively campaigning for their support both within the academic and larger outside community environments.

8. Branding of the university career services department in the international arena is a responsibility that all must understand and share.

Another commonly held notion is the branding of the university's career services department in the international arena. The institution as a brand, whose reputation (good and bad) is built primarily by the people who make up its entire or extended community, including creative faculty, loyal students, proud alumni, committed partners, and visionary administrators, is a key factor. Such people tend to be guided by the principle that a university's global standing is a product of the relationships it has with its extended constituencies.

These relationships were considered equal in value to a university's infrastructure or its ultimate product, namely, education itself. The more successful, globally focused universities tended to be those that proactively harnessed the emotional as well as the intellectual connections with all members of their extended communities. Such universities articulated worthy causes, communicated important outcomes, and promised meaningful experiences worthy of one's energies, time, and allegiance. In other words, among great universities, an overarching reality is that success is not just about the education (the product), or the buildings (the infrastructure), it is about the people and services (like career services).

Conclusion

Two concluding insights from this work can be offered. The first relates to perhaps the most profound hallmark of the new millennium—the ever-increasing interdependence of our world. Globalization is here, it is not going away, and those who embrace it will benefit the most. The second insight is that a good portion, if not the majority, of any institution of higher education's success comes from the people who develop, nurture, manage, and grow from the international experience offered by the institution. Career services departments that understand this, and can implement programs and partner with others to do this work, are likely to be out in front in terms of global preeminence.

References

Altbach, P. G., & McGill Peterson, P. (1998). Internationalize American higher education? Not exactly. *Change, 30*(4), 36–39.

Benedict-Augustin, A. (2010). *The impact of international internships on undergraduate college students' career development* (Unpublished doctoral dissertation). University of Pennsylvania, Philadelphia.

Bennett, J., & Salonen, R. (2007, March/April). Intercultural communication and the new American campus. *Change: The Magazine of Higher Learning, 39*(7), 46–50.

British University North American Club (BUNAC). (2012). Retrieved from http://www .bunac.org/usa

Cornwell, G. H., & Stoddard, E. W. (2006, Spring). Freedom, diversity, and global citizenship. *Liberal Education.* Retrieved from http://www.aacu.org/liberaleducation/ le-sp06/le-sp06_feature3.cfm

Evanson, T. A., & Zust, B. L. (2004). The meaning of participation in an international service experience among baccalaureate nursing students. *International Journal of Nursing Education Scholarship, 1*(1), 1–14.

Furnham, A., & Bockner, S. (1986). *Cultural shock: Psychological reactions to unfamiliar environments.* New York, NY: Methuen.

Green, M. F. (2012). *Global citizenship: What are we talking about and why does it matter?* Washington, DC: NAFSA. Retrieved from http://international.uiowa.edu/accents/

post/global-citizenship-%E2%80%93-what-are-we-talking-about-and-why-does-it
-matter

Green, M. F. (2014). *Measuring internationalization at research universities: The unifying voice for higher education.* Washington, DC: American Council on Education. Retrieved from http://www.acenet.edu/news-room/Documents/Measuring-Research.pdf

IHRM: International Human Resource Management. (2011). *Global talent management and global talent challenges: Strategic opportunities for IHRM.* Retrieved from http://www.shrm.org/hrdisciplines/global/pages/default.aspx

Institute for International Education (IIE). (2009). *Open Doors 2009: Report on international education exchange.* New York, NY: Author.

Jones, S. R., Rowan-Kenyon, H. T., Ireland, S. M., Niehaus, E., & Skendall, K. C. (2012). The meaning students make as participants in short-term immersion programs. *Journal of College Student Development, 53,* 201–220.

Lundstrom, W. J., White, D. S., & Schuster, C. P. (1996). Internationalizing the marketing curriculum: The professional marketer's perspective. *Journal of Marketing Education, 18*(7), 4–16.

Morais, D. B., & Ogdan, A. C. (2011). Initial development and validation of the global citizenship scale. *Journal of Studies in International Education, 15*(5), 445–466.

NAFSA: Association of International Educators. (2003). *Securing America's future: Global education for a global age.* Report of the strategic task force on education abroad. Washington, DC: Author. Retrieved from http://www.nafsa.org/uploadedFiles/NAFSA_Home/Resource_Library_Assets/Public_Policy/securing_america_s_future.pdf?n=3894

Nolan, P. (2009). *Transforming China: globalization, transition and development.* London, UK: Anthem.

Nolting, T. (2008). *An analysis of study abroad administration at U.S. colleges and universities.* Knoxville: University of Tennessee.

Reinholt, B. (2012). *International internships: A give and take affair.* Association Internationale des Étudiants en Sciences Économiques et Commerciales (AIESEC). Retrieved from https://www.eng.vt.edu/sites/default/files/pageattachments/international internships-agiveandtakeaffair.pdf

Richard, K. (2013). *Global citizenship and the university: Advancing social life and relations in an interdependent world.* Stanford, CA: Stanford University Press.

Rowan-Kenyon, H. T., & Niehaus, E. K. (2011). One year later: The influence of short-term study abroad experiences on students. *Journal of Student Affairs Research and Practice, 48,* 213–228.

Stier, J. (2003). Internationalization, ethnic diversity and the acquisition of intercultural competencies. *Intercultural Education, 14*(1), 77–91.

MARK A. KENYON *is the director for the Office of Career Services and Internships at University of Massachusetts Boston.*

HEATHER T. ROWAN-KENYON *is an associate professor of higher education at Boston College.*

NEW DIRECTIONS FOR STUDENT SERVICES • DOI: 10.1002/ss

INDEX

CPSIA information can be obtained at www.ICGtesting.com
Printed in the USA
BVOW04s0544300615

406714BV00015B/244/P